MITCHELL BEAZLEY
DISCOVERING WINE COUNTRY

Bordeaux

Monty Waldin

D1010424

Series editor: Patrick Matthews

DISCOVERING WINE COUNTRY
BORDEAUX
by Monty Waldin

FIrst published in Great Britain in 2005
by Mitchell Beazley, an imprint of Octopus Publishing Group Limited,
2–4 Heron Quays, London E14 4JP.

A CIP catalogue record for this book is available from the British Library.

ISBN: 1 84533 038 2

The author and publishers will be grateful for any information which will assist them in keeping
future editions up-to-date. Although all reasonable care has been taken in the preparation of this
book, neither the publishers nor the author can accept any liability for any consequences arising
from the use thereof, or the information contained therein.

Photographs by Victoria McTernan
Map creation by Encompass Graphics

Commissioning Editor Hilary Lumsden
Executive Art Editor Yasia Williams-Leedham
Senior Designer Tim Pattinson
Managing Editor Julie Sheppard
Editor Margaret Rand
Designer Gaelle Lochner
Index Hilary Bird
Production Gary Hayes

Typeset in Futura and Sabon

Printed and bound by Toppan Printing Company in China

Contents

How to use this book

Discovering Wine Country is all about getting you from the page to the producer. Each chapter covers a specific winemaking region of interest, and includes a map of the area featured, with places of interest marked using the symbols below. The leading wine producers mentioned are all given a map grid reference so you can see exactly where they are.

The maps include key features to help you navigate your way round the routes, but they are not intended to replace detailed road maps, or indeed detailed vineyard maps, normally available from local tourist offices or the local wine bureau (*see* below right and p.89).

It wouldn't be practical to mark each and every grower on the maps. Instead the sign ❧ means that an area or village is home to at least one recommended wine producer. The wine regions covered are packed with other points of interest for the wine enthusiast but that are unrelated to actual wine purchasing. These are shown as ♜ Sometimes this includes growers who don't sell direct but whose status is such that they will be on any wine-lover's itinerary. Exceptional restaurants are marked ¡Ol and towns and villages where there's an Office de Tourism are marked **i** which is especially useful for finding *gîtes* and campsites.

Quick reference map symbols
❧ recommended wine producer
♜ wine tourist site
★ tourist attraction
¡Ol recommended restaurant
i tourist information centre

☐ named wine region

▬▬ author's suggested wine route(s) to follow, with information
about how long the route is and any other useful tips.

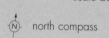 scale bar

Ⓝ north compass

Boxed information

☐ the contact details of hotels, restaurants, tourist information, hire shops, transport facilities, and other points of interest.

☐ wine-related information as well as the author's selection of the top growers to visit in the specific area featured, including contact details, a map reference, and a price indicator:
inexpensive: <€5
moderate: €5–10
expensive: €10–20

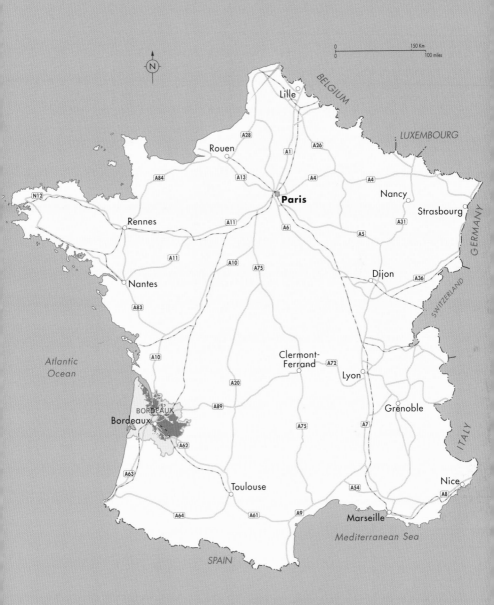

150 Km

100 miles

BELGIUM

LUXEMBOURG

GERMANY

SWITZERLAND

ITALY

SPAIN

Atlantic Ocean

Mediterranean Sea

Lille

Rouen

Paris

Nancy

Strasbourg

Rennes

Nantes

Dijon

Clermont-Ferrand

Lyon

Grenoble

BORDEAUX
Bordeaux

Toulouse

Nice

Marseille

N12
A28
A1
A26
A84
A13
A4
A4
N12
A11
A31
A6
A5
A11
A10
A75
A36
A83
A10
A72
A20
A89
A75
A7
A62
A63
A54
A8
A64
A61
A9

Local wine bureau

CIVB (Conseil Interprofessionnel
du Vin de Bordeaux),
www.vins-bordeaux.fr

Introduction

Travelling around the world's biggest and arguably best wine region is daunting because of the number of châteaux to visit, but unforgettable because almost wherever you go you'll see a sign to a world-famous winery. I remember arriving at Libourne railway station back in 1984 for my first visit to Bordeaux. I was a teenager, and I'd been on the train from my home in southern England for nearly twenty-four hours. I was so tired I almost missed the stop, but I vividly recall the August heat hitting me even at 11pm as the train doors opened.

A summer of swotting

RIGHT *An equally impeccable vineyard (see p.46).*

BELOW *The houses along the Bordeaux waterfront have been impeccably spruced up in recent years.*

Soon I was in the back of a beaten-up Renault hurtling towards my destination, a small château in Entre-Deux-Mers, where I was due to spend the summer learning French. My French teacher had suggested, in fact ordered, that I spend some time in France if I was to avert a disaster in my forthcoming oral examinations. A schoolfriend's father had got me a job gardening for the summer. But I had no idea that this would prove to be my start in the wine trade. It turned out that my employer had turned his hand to wine broking, so I ended up

working in the vineyards, too. After work, I started reading wine magazines and books, and one night had a stroke of luck that was to change my life. A tasting had been organized for a prospective client and I was invited. Three vintages of the same wine, a St-Emilion, were shown blind. I managed to guess all three right.

Falling in love

I realised that wine was not such a strange, amorphous subject. Besides, I loved the Bordeaux climate, which was hot but rarely stifling, and I loved Bordeaux food. The girls seemed more exotic, too, than my contemporaries at school, which for a lustful (if not lusty) teenager was a major bonus. But above all else I loved the wines. When I went back to school I would infuriate my friends who wanted to get in and out of wine shops on illegal booze-buying trips as quickly as possible. I would pace the aisles weighing up the relative merits of this château or that appellation, this vintage year and that price. But I would always choose a Bordeaux.

Be picky – you're the buyer

What I learnt about Bordeaux is that no wine region on earth gives you such a wide choice. As a visitor and a potential buyer you are in the driving-seat, so make sure you give your time and your money to producers you like and whose wines you want to drink. Don't ever feel that you should part with your cash just because you are in a grand château.

This book is aimed both at those who know a lot about wine but have never been to Bordeaux, and at those who know a little and want to explore. I have focused on lesser châteaux because that's what most of us can afford to buy, but this book tells you how to visit the great ones too.

Experiencing the real Bordeaux

Use this book in conjunction with general guide books and detailed road maps to find your way around. You will get lost – everybody does in Bordeaux – but you'll find the people are generally helpful to visitors. You won't forget your trip. It is the place wine-lovers always talk about: to swap tasting experiences, to moan about prices or to congratulate you on getting a bargain, or to compare real Bordeaux with those thousands of producers worldwide who try to copy its inimitable style. Bordeaux is an awesome place, but don't be overawed by it.

Understanding
Bordeaux

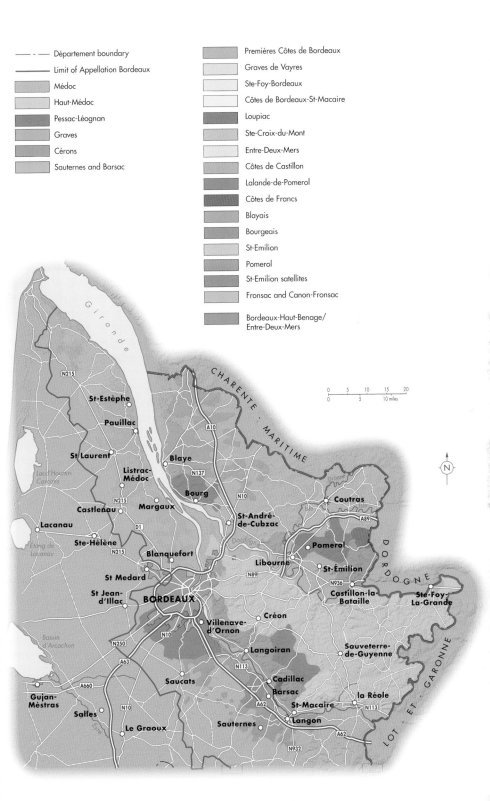

Département boundary
Limit of Appellation Bordeaux
Médoc
Haut-Médoc
Pessac-Léognan
Graves
Cérons
Sauternes and Barsac

Premières Côtes de Bordeaux
Graves de Vayres
Ste-Foy-Bordeaux
Côtes de Bordeaux-St-Macaire
Loupiac
Ste-Croix-du-Mont
Entre-Deux-Mers
Côtes de Castillon
Lalande-de-Pomerol
Côtes de Francs
Blayais
Bourgeais
St-Emilion
Pomerol
St-Emilion satellites
Fronsac and Canon-Fronsac
Bordeaux-Haut-Benage/
Entre-Deux-Mers

Why Bordeaux makes great wines

I t is often said that quality and quantity are incompatible, but Bordeaux proves to be Planet Wine's outstanding exception. It is both the world's biggest wine region and home to what many consider are the world's greatest wines. It has also been the inspiration for many great and not-so-great look-alikes, from France and elsewhere.

Collectability

The private cellars of all serious wine producers, and most serious wine-lovers, will contain bottles of Bordeaux. These wines combine everything: they are full of flavour but are not overpowering, they refresh the taste-buds and make one eager for the next sip, and they are easily digestible. You could sum up by saying that Bordeaux's greatest quality is elegance. So where does this elegance come from? Well, there's no simple answer, but elegance comes from a combination of Bordeaux's geography, its soils and climate, and the kind of grapes used to make the wines.

RIGHT *Gravel soils are perfect in Bordeaux's damp climate.*

BELOW *The tower at Château Latour: one of Bordeaux's most famous landmarks.*

Growing slowly

First of all, Bordeaux has a long growing season, which means the grapes ripen slowly enough to build up lots of flavour. Bordeaux's climate is warm-to-hot, but not so torrid that all the flavours in the grapes get burnt out by the sun. One key influence is the huge Landes forests that lie between the vineyards and the Atlantic ocean; the other is the ocean itself. Forest and sea combine to moderate excess summer heat. Conveniently, they also prevent Bordeaux from getting really cold, and years like 1956 and 1985, when frosts were harsh enough to kill vines, are rare. Of course, the downside of having an ocean on the doorstep is that Bordeaux is one of the world's wetter wine regions. Vines hate having wet feet, especially late ripeners like Cabernet Sauvignon.

Perfect soil

The miracle of Bordeaux – and it really is a miracle – is the soil. It is described locally as "*filtrant*" or easily self-draining, as the rain quickly runs away through what is generally fine-textured sandy gravel on the Left Bank, and soft limestone on the Right Bank.

The gravel was washed down from the Pyrénées when the glaciers melted between three and five million years ago. As well as being free-draining, it allows vine roots to plunge deep into the subsoil where they can find complex mineral elements that help give the finest wines their complex, undefinable flavours. The gravel also acts like a night-storage-heater, trapping the warmth of the sun during the day and reflecting it back onto the grapes at night, helping to ripen the skins.

Seeing starfish

The soft limestone of the Right Bank was formed around 650,000 years ago out of what was a seabed. It was the last resting place of billions of tiny sea creatures whose starfish shape means that growers on the Right Bank (especially in Fronsac and St-Emilion) often talk of "starfish limestone" (*calcaire à astéries*).

Limestone comes into its own in hot years, for it acts like a sponge. It sucks up rainwater, releasing it slowly to the vines during the hottest weather. Without this the vine would shut down for critical periods in very hot weather, and the grapes would not be ripe by the time late autumn rains and cold weather brought the season to a close.

Luck and good judgement

The Bordeaux wine-growers are fortunate in having such fine raw materials. But they have worked hard in matching their chosen grape varieties to the subtle variations in the soils, and have learnt that the best wines in Bordeaux are blends of more than one grape.

Securing the market

Yet they are ruthless too. In the middle ages Bordeaux granted itself the "great privilege" of refusing to sell the "high country" red wines of Cahors until after Bordeaux's own stocks had run dry. The Bordelais simply blocked the Garonne down which the Cahors wines would travel by barge – or they would blend Cahors' firm, dark reds into their own wines if the Bordeaux vintage had been a light one – but without, of course, giving Cahors any credit.

Bordeaux's capacity for self-promotion may be rivalled only by that of Champagne. The world's biggest wine fair, Vinexpo, is staged here – but Bordeaux has also helped create other great wine industries,.

When French vineyards were devastated by mildew and phylloxera in the nineteenth century, the Bordelais invested massively in finding solutions. But, they also took cuttings from their vines to northern Spain and Chile, for example, spawning Bordeaux-style red wines that are still made there today. As any Bordelais will tell you, imitation is the finest form of flattery.

BORDEAUX WINE FACTS

Bordeaux has nearly **120,000ha of vines**, more than the whole of Germany or Chile, three and a half times as much as Champagne, and four times as much as Burgundy.

Bordeaux produces **850 million bottles a year**, or one in four bottles of all French *appellation contrôlée* wine.

Bordeaux has **fifty-seven appellations contrôlées**.

It has **10,000 wine-producing châteaux**, fifty-three cooperatives, 130 wine brokers or middlemen, and 400 merchants.

Eighty per cent of its wine is red, seventeen per cent is dry white, and three per cent is sweet white. A small amount of sparkling wine and rosé are made, too.

Bordeaux people

S oil and climate are crucial for wine, but we should not forget about the people behind the wines, too. In Bordeaux, you'll be hard-pressed to find someone with absolutely no involvement in wine. Yes, fishing, forestry and tourism are important motors for the Bordeaux economy, but here wine is king.

Mass involvement

The region has over 20,000 wine businesses – grape-growers, wineries, cooperatives, merchants, and brokers, plus suppliers of vineyard machinery, bottles, wooden cases, labels, and corks.

But, Bordeaux became rich on more than just wine. During the eighteenth century, for example, trade with France's colonies in sugar, cocoa, and slaves dominated the port.

The wealth generated was invested by Bordeaux's emerging landed gentry in cultivating political favours at Court and in building châteaux and planting large-scale vineyards. In contrast, wine-growers in Burgundy, for example, have relatively small, scattered vineyard-holdings. The reason is that much of the Côte d'Or was owned by the Church until the Revolution, and sold to smallholders when the Church was dispossessed. The Church was never a large landowner in Bordeaux.

Hands off

And this brings us to another difference between Burgundy and Bordeaux. In Burgundy, the winery owner does much of the

vineyard work himself, be it fixing the tractor or pruning. In Bordeaux, the grandest owners will only ever get their hands dirty if they spill the ink in their fountain pens. All the manual labour is left to hired help.

Indeed, the families who own the top 200 or 300

châteaux in the Medoc's flagship regions like Pauillac, Margaux, and St-Julien often don't live on-site, but prefer to reside in the upmarket suburbs of Bordeaux, with Le Bouscat being particularly handy for the D1 and D2.

In contrast, château owners in St-Emilion, Pomerol, and Entre-Deux-Mers tend to live at their properties, and are more hands-on with their approach. Some even work on the bottling lines in the sweltering August heat if the pressure is on to empty the vats of last year's crop as September and the next harvest approaches.

The importance of lunch

The working day in Bordeaux, as in France, is still fairly regimented, and revolves around meals. The French live to eat whereas others eat to live.

Most working winery owners start at 8am and work to midday, take a two-hour lunch and then work another four hours in the afternoon. In theory, French employees only work a thirty-five hour week now, but the reality can be different.

ABOVE *Oysters near Archachon – this time in painted form, on a door.*

LEFT Boules *beside the river: agreeable even on a chilly day.*

Social life is most active in the bigger towns, such as Bordeaux, Langon, and Libourne, but, in the backwoods villages of the southern Graves, the northern Blayais, and Entre-Deux-Mers the streets are deserted as night falls.

Status symbols vary, too. While in the more humdrum vineyards, growers will be keen to show off a new tractor or a fancy wine press to their neighbours, at the top châteaux the owners will carefully drop into conversation the names of the politicians or pop stars who came to dinner last night.

Wine from the top chateaux is bought by Bordeaux merchants or "negociants" via intermediaries called brokers or "courtiers". The merchants trade the wine between themselves and foreign merchants until it finds its way into shops, restaurants, and private cellars. This system is unique to Bordeaux, and means you can't buy top Bordeaux direct from the château. In years when demand for top Bordeaux is strong or when the harvest is small, the châteaux owners have the whip-hand. In years when money is tight and production is large, the négociants have the better bargaining position. For consumers, the ideal is to buy top Bordeaux from great vintages when the market is slack because, put simply, this is when you get more bangs for your bucks.

Seasons and festivals

Part of the fun of visiting a winery is to go out into the vineyards. The only time when absolutely nothing is going on in the vines is just after harvest, usually September and October. By November, once most of the leaves have fallen, pruning begins. The vine needs to be cut back partly to stop the vineyard becoming a jungle, but also to control the size of the following year's crop. Pruning can continue all through the winter, but must be completed by the spring.

March to April

It takes one man roughly three to four weeks to prune one hectare of vines. Then, as the soil warms up, the buds burst, and new green shoots start growing. By late April these shoots are high enough to need to be tied to supporting wires.

June flowers

In June, the vines flower. A period of dry, fine and not-too-windy weather will ensure a good fruit-set. This can be a good time to visit Bordeaux, as the weather is usually good and the vineyards are lush and full of promise.

One hundred days of summer

It is said to be 100 days from flowering to the start of the harvest, and usually it is, more or less. However, it is only during August that the small, hard, green berries begin to swell, soften, and change colour – to golden-yellow in the case of white varieties and dark purple in the case of reds. The first two weeks of August are the worst time to visit wineries as very few proprietors will be there. This is the most popular fortnight in the French calendar for an annual holiday. Things get back to normal by the beginning of September when wineries are a flurry of activity.

Preparation time

Bottling often takes place now, to empty the vats of last year's crop ready for the new intake. Presses, pumps, and hoses needed to be cleaned; food organized for an army of pickers; and machine harvesters dusted down and checked.

Once harvest starts it can be difficult to arrange winery visits. Many châteaux stop receiving visitors.

Party time

The French authorities prosecute wineries who hire pickers without the right papers, so don't expect to be able to pick. But, if you do get the papers and join in, you'll have sticky fingers and a sore back but the promise of a superb harvest lunch waiting for you if you make it through the morning. There's usually a party for the pickers after the harvest, too. Your fellow pickers will also teach you some new French words – usually ones not listed in the dictionary. *Bonne chance*!

When to visit

The sunniest months are June, July, and August – August being the hottest – which average over 230 hours of sunshine each. Avoid January if you hate the cold, as average temperatures drop to a low of around 9°C (48°F) which, while not exactly freezing, chills the bones more than you might think, thanks to Bordeaux's natural humidity. Likewise, avoid December if you hate the rain, as this is usually the wettest month.

ABOVE *There's no escaping oyster shells in Bordeaux.*

When to stay at home

The world's biggest wine trade fair, Vinexpo, takes place in Bordeaux every other year (2005, 2007, and so on). Wine merchants, wine producers, and the wine media from all over the world descend on Bordeaux. Accommodation becomes very hard to find; restaurant and bar prices seem to creep up, and traffic in and around Bordeaux city is nightmarish. You have been warned!

LEFT *There's a merry-go-round in the centre of Bordeaux, for a different view of the city.*

BELOW *Sunset over the Pont de Pierre, Bordeaux city's most beautiful bridge.*

Knowing the wines

Although Bordeaux is the biggest fine-wine region in the world there is no need to feel overwhelmed by it. True, there are around 10,000 châteaux, all making different wines, not to mention the myriad brands produced by the region's cooperatives and négociants; but in terms of styles of wine there is nothing to fear. Most of the world's most familiar wine styles are made in Bordeaux: dry reds, dry whites, sweet or "dessert" whites, and pink wines, plus white and pink sparkling wines.

ABOVE *The most ageable wines are sold in wooden boxes.*

RIGHT *Bordeaux's vineyards are gently undulating rather than flat.*

Get your bearings

The first thing to do to understand this geographically massive region is to break it down into more manageable segments. So, imagine the Bordeaux region as a clock-face, with the city of Bordeaux at the centre.

From midnight to six are the regions of the Right Bank – the bank in question being that of the rivers Garonne and Gironde. From six to midnight are those of the Left Bank: you will hear people talking of "Right Bank" wines or "Left Bank" wines. Understanding the differences between the Left Bank and the Right Bank will really help you get to grips with Bordeaux and all its nuances.

Left or Right?

The main Left Bank sub-regions are the Médoc, Pessac-Léognan and Graves, and Barsac-Sauternes. The main Right Bank sub-regions are Bourg and Blaye, the Libournais areas of St-Emilion, Pomerol and Fronsac, and Entre-Deux-Mers.

Four out of five bottles of Bordeaux contain red, and generally speaking the Left Bank favours the later ripening Cabernet Sauvignon, while the Right Bank has earlier ripening grapes like Merlot and Cabernet Franc. There's a very good reason for this.

Gravel to the Left

On the Left Bank the soils are generally gravelly, which Cabernet Sauvignon prefers. It is often said to hate "getting its feet wet". The loose, gravelly soils of the Médoc, and Pessac-Léognan and Graves, drain well; the fact that the Left Bank's gravel is interspersed with lots of sand also helps drainage. And well-drained soils are warmer than wet ones, thus helping Cabernet Sauvignon to ripen: important for such a late-ripening variety.

But hang on; you could say that if the Left Bank's gravelly sand is so good for Cabernet Sauvignon, why is the Left Bank also so well known for the dry whites of Pessac-Léognan, which are picked up to a month before Cabernet Sauvignon, not to mention the late-picked, sweet white wines of Sauternes-Barsac, which can be picked up to a month after Cabernet Sauvignon?

It's a fair point, to which the answer is this: soils are never uniform, something wine-growers worked out long before geologists came along. Over the centuries Bordeaux's growers have, through trial and error, discovered which grapes work best in each plot of land. It turns out that where the Left Bank soils drain less well, for instance where sticky, water-retaining clay is mixed in with the sand and gravel, the grapes which flourish are Sauvignon Blanc and Sémillon for dry whites. Sauvignon Blanc planted on the most gravelly soils would certainly ripen, but it would ripen too well and quickly become overripe, losing its aroma and freshness.

As far as the sweet white wines of Sauternes-Barsac and Cérons are concerned, while the soil type is important perhaps the most crucial factor is the local microclimate, in other words the effect the river mists have in shrivelling already-ripened grapes to make them extra-sweet (see p.91 for details of how this process works).

Storage heaters

Vines on the Left Bank are planted close together, sometimes at densities as high as 10,000 vines per hectare, although a figure of 7,500 vines per hectare is more usual. These high

densities are because the soils here are quite poor. Low-vigour soils like these tend to produce smaller vines, and wine quality is improved if the vines are crowded together, forcing them to compete for scarce resources.

The crucial thing for wine quality is not the yield per hectare, but the yield per vine. For reds and dry whites on the Left Bank, growers can produce about 8,000 bottles per hectare, or about one bottle per vine per year.

Left Bank vines are trained low to the ground, partly again because small vines suit poor soils, but also because the gravel reflects heat back onto the grapes during the day, thus speeding the ripening process. At night, the gravel acts as a heat store, again helping the grapes to ripen.

Clay to the Right

On the Right Bank it is a different story. Here the soils are dominated by clay in the topsoil, and limestone or sandstone underneath. These types of soils favour earlier-ripening red grapes like Merlot and Cabernet Franc, and white grapes. Why? It's a question of drainage again. Limestone can be quite water-retentive, and clay always is, and the wetter the soil the colder it is. Soils like this take time to warm up in spring, and cool quickly in autumn, meaning that late-ripeners like Cabernet Sauvignon will rarely perform as well as vines like Merlot and Cabernet Franc which bud and ripen up to two weeks earlier than Cabernet Sauvignon.

You can squeeze a piece of clay as hard as you like and it will still feel damp to the touch. Soils that hold water like this can also hold nutrients. This means that Right Bank vines grow bigger than their counterparts on the Left Bank, and are allowed to grow higher from the ground. This helps protect the bunches from humidity which can invite fungal diseases like mildew and rot. The vines also need to be spaced further apart to allow them room to spread out. Cramping vines in high-vigour soils leads to too much shading of the grapes, which in turn leads to less ripeness.

RIGHT *A deep colour can be a sign of very ripe grapes.*

BELOW *Sticky hands are a problem, come the harvest.*

On the Right Bank vines are planted at densities of around 5,000 vines per hectare. Each vine is thus producing nearly one and a half bottles each year, compared to about a bottle on the other side of the river. Does that mean that wines from the Right Bank are not as good as those from the Left Bank, because Right Bank vines have to produce more wine per vine?

Not at all. It's all about the vines being in balance. Vines on the Left Bank are happy to produce what they do, and vines on the Right

Bank are just as happy to produce slightly more each year, on their richer, higher vigour soils.

The best wines from limestone soils are intense, smooth, and elegant, like velvet across the tongue. The best wines from gravel-dominated soils are powerful, rich, and mouth-filling.

Ingredients

The main wine grape varieties in Bordeaux for pink and red wines are Merlot, Cabernet Sauvignon, and Cabernet Franc, with Malbec, Petit Verdot, and Carmenère also grown in small amounts.

For white wines, whether dry, sweet, still or sparkling, the main grapes are Sauvignon Blanc and Sémillon, with Muscadelle, Ugni Blanc, Colombard, and Sauvignon Gris also planted. See below for profiles of these grape varieties.

Reds and sweet whites in Bordeaux are almost always a blend of two or more varieties; dry whites may be either a blend or a single varietal.

Grape flavours: the main red varieties

Cabernet Franc is a red grape related to Cabernet Sauvignon, but slightly earlier ripening. Its wine smells of violets and can be exotic, but can also be weedy-tasting when overcropped. It's a chameleon, performing well on both Left and Right Banks, but on the Left Bank is generally regarded as the lesser of the two Cabernets, providing elegance and aroma to the blend. It is refreshing without being tart.

Cabernet Sauvignon, is the better-known big brother of Cabernet Franc. A red grape with small berries, it has a pungent blackcurrant smell and flavour to its wine, turning to cedar and cigar-boxes with age. Its wines have crisp mouthfeel, with firm tannins and structure, but plenty of flavour and a dark colour, too. This is what Cabernet Sauvignon brings to any blend.

Key regions for the variety are Pauillac, St-Julien, and Pessac-Léognan.

Merlot is fast becoming even better known worldwide than Cabernet Sauvignon, and it's certainly being planted more and more in Bordeaux, even on the Left Bank. Its wines taste of plum and Christmas cake, or even redcurrant jelly and menthol, and these rich, easy flavours have great appeal to wine-drinkers. Its wines have a soft, fleshy texture, which also goes down well with modern wine drinkers, and this softness and fleshiness can fill out the leaner, tougher profile of Cabernet Sauvignon or the leaner and more delicate structure of Cabernet Franc. Its wine is earlier maturing than Cabernet Sauvignon, too; another plus point on the market. The grapes are early ripening, so can deal with the cool clay soils of the Right Bank.

Key regions are Pomerol and St-Emilion.

The lesser-known red grape varieties

Malbec is the widest planted of the lesser-known reds, but only ever forms a small part of the blend. It's a red variety found sporadically in St-Emilion, where it is called Côt, and more often in Bourg and Blaye. Malbec's big, round, and slightly red leaves resemble its soft, moderately crimson wines. It tastes of cracked pepper in cool years, tar in warmer ones.

Petit Verdot is a red grape grown in only small quantities in Bordeaux. It has thick skins that ripen with difficulty, even on the warmest, most gravel-rich Left Bank vineyards. However, dedicated growers in Margaux and St-Julien are returning to Petit Verdot, as a small percentage can add a soft, tarry texture to Cabernet Sauvignon-dominated blends.

Carmenère is a very minor red grape in Bordeaux. A small percentage is very occasionally used to season the odd Left

Bank red, but it yields erratically. This erratic habit has been its downfall in Bordeaux: before phylloxera it was very highly regarded here and widely planted, but it didn't take happily to being grafted, and growers abandoned it. It has good, exotic flavours of Turkish delight at its best, but is often flavourless and astringent at its overcropped worst.

White varieties: the big two

Sauvignon Blanc is the most widely planted of Bordeaux's fair-skinned varieties. Unripe Sauvignon tastes of cat's pee, but when ripe it adds pungent nettle and fresh grass flavours to dry whites.

Key regions are Pessac-Léognan, Graves, Entre-Deux-Mers, and Premières Côtes de Bordeaux. Also used in sweet whites, often comprising up to a quarter.

Sémillon is a fair-skinned grape with speckled, golden berries. It produces soft, dry whites with a texture of churned butter, and lush, honeyed, sweet whites when affected by noble rot.

Key regions are Pessac-Léognan, Graves, Entre-Deux-Mers, Premières Côtes de Bordeaux, Barsac, and Sauternes.

The rest of the white varieties

Muscadelle is grown for dry whites in the hilly Premières Côtes de Bordeaux. It also has a role in Sauternes-Barsac, where a tiny percentage in the blend can give a lift to the flavour of Sémillon and Sauvignon Blanc. It buds late and ripens early, and has the shortest growing cycle of all the Bordeaux grapes. The berries contain only a single pip; two to four pips are more common in other varieties. Muscadelle has attractive musky tastes mixed with barley and citrus.

Colombard is a fair-skinned variety producing big berries with thin skins that are popular with wasps. It survives in Entre-Deux-Mers and Blaye, but its slightly herbal, crisp, ephemeral wine is used mainly to fill out merchant blends of no particular distinction. It is not used for fine wine in Bordeaux

Sauvignon Gris is a pink-skinned version of Sauvignon Blanc, and can give a powerful musky sheen to a very small number of white wines in Premières Côtes de Bordeaux, Graves, and Pessac-Léognan. It's less pungent than its white cousin. It's that rare thing: a wine grape that can also serve as a table grape.

Ugni Blanc produces bucketloads of crisp, flavourless wine, mainly in Blaye and some other Right Bank regions.

ABOVE *Without leaves to capture sunlight, vines cannot ripen their grapes.*

LEFT *The offices of the Bordeaux Wine Bureau (CIVB, see p.5), centrally located on the Cours du XXX Juillet.*

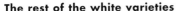

Food and wine culture

T he unifying cultural forces in Bordeaux consist of a love-hate relationship with the English, and a passion for wine and gastronomy. The love-hate relationship, as every Bordeaux schoolchild knows, stems from when the English took possession of this part of France in 1152, when its feudal overlord, Eleanor of Acquitaine, married the future Henry II of England. The 1453 Battle of Castillon ended English rule, but ever since 1152 the English have been Bordeaux's best foreign customer, give or take the odd moment of trading difficulty because of war.

Local produce

Bordeaux is often seen by the rest of France as something of a gastronomic backwater, but you will eat well here. Just don't expect to encounter the rich, creamy sauces of Normandy or the offal- and potato-based cuisine of Lyon. From March to June asparagus is in season. The Blaye region is Bordeaux's main area for asparagus production. It is usually steamed, with olive oil, vinaigrette or hollandaise sauce. Try with simple dry whites like Entre-Deux-Mers or Bordeaux Blanc Sec.

"Le plat"

Main course options revolve around beef, lamb, fish, or fowl. The most common beef dish is *entrecôte à la Bordelaise*, or ribsteak with Bordelaise sauce. The meat is usually oiled, salted, and grilled on vine prunings (*sarments de vigne*). The sauce is based on red wine over a roux of melted butter and flour, and meat stock with finely chopped shallots, and garlic. A simpler variation, *entrecôte aux echalottes*, is steak grilled with a covering of raw shallots. Look out for leg of lamb (*gigot d'agneau*), usually served rare, with salt-marsh Pauillac lamb a speciality. Slivers of garlic are inserted into the meat before it goes in the oven. Beef and lamb are perfect with any red Bordeaux

Duck for dinner

Duck is a common main course, in the form of either *magret de canard*, a lean duck breast from a bird that has produced foie gras or the much richer *confit de canard.*– ultra-tender duck leg cooked and stored in its own fat, then crisped in a hot oven. *Confit d'oie*, the same thing but made from goose, is even richer

and more highly flavoured. Try with rich Merlot-based reds such as St-Emilion and Pomerol. You might be served locally farmed, trapped or shot quail (*caille*), bunting (*ortolan*), turtle dove (*touterelle*), and wood pigeon stew (*salmis de palombe*).

A surfeit of lampreys

The most famous fish dish in Bordeaux is lamprey (*lamproie a la bordelaise*). This leech-like fish is caught locally between April and May, and is prepared by stewing it for several hours in red wine, with leeks. The bony shad (*alose*) is usually cooked slowly to soften its bones and is typically served garnished with sage. Try with full-bodied dry whites from Graves and Pessac-Léognan. Grilled eels (*anguilles grillées*) are a favourite during summer and autumn, as are elvers (*piballes*). Local seafood dishes favour lobster and crayfish, and Arcachon oysters (best from September to December), which can be served with small sausages and Gironde-produced caviar (*see* www.caviaraquitaine.com).

Mushrooms

Cèpes (*Boletus edulis*) are a delicacy and a common garnish, especially with omelette. The local type is a black (*tête de noir*) or brown-headed boletus, collected wild from July to early November, and chewy in texture unless well cooked. Best oven-baked, stuffed with sausage and a drop of armagnac, but are usually served *à la Bordelaise* with butter, garlic, and parsley.

A paucity of cheese

Bordeaux is one of the few French regions without a recognized native cheese. You might be offered mimolette, a hard, dark-orange cheese that is nothing more exotic than a mature Edam look-alike, but which goes well with reds or medium-dry whites.

ABOVE *Removing excess shoots by hand, early in the season.*

LEFT *Signs advertising "dégustation gratuite" or free wine tastings are the best way of getting potential shoppers through the door.*

BELOW *The Quai des Chartons is the traditional home of Bordeaux's wine merchants.*

How to get there

Bordeaux is France's second city and so is well served by various transport links. Since it is also a major port – indeed this was one reason the local wine became so well known in England and Holland from the twelfth century onwards – you can easily reach many of the wine regions by boat.

By water

Sailors have two main destinations. The first is the harbour at Archachon (www.port-arcachon.com), 80km (50 miles) due west of Bordeaux on the Atlantic coast. From here it's an hour's drive across the Landes forests to reach the Médoc vineyards, or two hours-plus for St-Emilion and Pomerol on the Right Bank. Bypass the centre of Bordeaux with the ring road, the Rocade.

The second option is to sail up the Gironde estuary and into the port of Bordeaux's enclosed docks (*bassins-flots*) for pleasure craft, near the town centre. There are various nautical stopping places on the way in to Bordeaux, for example at Le Verdon on the tip of the Médoc peninsula, in Pauillac for the central Médoc, and at Blaye for the Blayais on the opposite side.

Masted boats will not be able to pass under the Pont de Pierre in Bordeaux to penetrate the river Garonne, and the bridge at Libourne is the limit for those on the river Dordogne. On the Dordogne one can stop at Bourg, confusingly called Bourg-sur-Gironde, when in fact it lies on the Dordogne.

BELOW *St-Emilion's Chateau Ausone is named after a Roman consul, Ausonius.*

RIGHT *Gustave Eiffel built bridges at both Branne and Castillon-la-Bataille.*

By air

The recent growth of no-frills airlines in Europe has made Bordeaux a much cheaper place to fly to. Bordeaux has an international airport, Bordeaux-Mérignac (tel: 05 56 34 50 50, www.bordeaux.aeroport. fr). This is located 12km (7.5 miles) west of Bordeaux city, taking exits 11a or 11b off the Rocade. The Jet-Bus coach shuttle between city and airport takes thirty minutes. Mérignac is handy for the Left Bank.

Alternatively, you can fly to Bergerac-Roumanières (tel: 05 53 22 25 25, www.pays-de-bergerac.com). From here it is one hour's drive along the Bergerac-Libourne D936 to

reach St-Emilion, about the same time as it would take from Bordeaux-Mérignac. Leave the D936 at Ste-Foy la Grande for easy access to the eastern part of the Entre-Deux-Mers.

Another regional airport worth considering is Périgueux, around ninety minutes' drive on the N89.

By train
Bordeaux's main train station, Gare St-Jean, is about 3km (2 miles) southeast of the city centre. It connects to Bayonne, Nantes, Poitiers, La Rochelle, Toulouse, Lille, and Paris.

France's state-owned railway system, the Société Nationale des Chemins de Fer or SNCF, is one of the most extensive and efficient in Europe. For train times and fares see www.voyages-sncf.com or www.sncf.com. The TGV journey from Paris to Libourne or Bordeaux Gare St-Jean takes three hours.

By road
Bordeaux is 877km (550 miles) from Calais, 810km (506 miles) from Lille, 648km (405 miles) from Cherbourg and 579km (362 miles) from Paris. French motorways are much quicker and safer than national roads (Routes Nationales or RN) but are subject to tolls. (See www.autoroutes.fr)

TIP FOR A QUICK TRIP

If heading to the Médoc when driving from the north of France, **avoid Bordeaux city by taking the ferry from Royan** (follow the N150 from the A10 Bordeaux-Paris motorway at Saintes) to Pointe de Grave-Le Verdon. The ferry runs every thirty-five minutes from 7am to 9.30pm and takes thirty minutes (tel: 05 46 38 35 15).

Where to stay

Y ou won't find yourselves short of accommodation options in Bordeaux – unless you chose to visit during the world's largest wine trade fair, Vinexpo (*see* p.14) when the region is at its busiest.

Bed and breakfast

Many of Bordeaux's smaller growers are in financial difficulty, thanks to the massive growth in the popularity of wines from Chile, Australia, South Africa, and New Zealand. One option smaller, family owned wineries are taking to generate income is to offer bed and breakfast or *"chambres d'hôte"*, literally (but don't expect too much literalness) "the bedroom of the host". The price of a continental breakfast is usually included in the price. You may also be offered ham, cheese, pâté, and yoghurt. Tea drinkers should note that your French hosts will be happy to give you what you need to make your tea, and won't be offended if you bring your own teabags. Some bed and breakfast establishments also offer an evening meal (*table d'hôte*).

Most bed and breakfast recommendations in this book are described as "average" in terms of price (from €40 and €70), based on two people sharing, with breakfast.

RIGHT *Gothic architecture in St-Emilion.*

BELOW *One of Bordeaux's many city centre hotels.*

Self-catering holiday homes or *gîtes*

Larger groups or families might consider renting a holiday home or an apartment, called a *gîte* in French, a word which literally means "shelter". It's impossible to generalize about where the prettiest ones are to be found in Bordeaux, as architectural styles vary widely across the region. They are usually either purpose-built houses, or have been converted from farm or winery outbuildings.

Location, location, location

Location is key, and is the biggest influence on price. What you need to consider is whether you just want a simple base, with washing machine (*machine à laver*) for example, or if you want to play host during your stay and have big family meals. If the latter, you need to find out how far away are the nearest shops and markets, and when they open. Some backwoods villages have produce suppliers delivering essentials like bread, for example, two or three times a week.

Also check whether yours is the only *gîte* on larger properties, and if so if facilities like gardens, swimming pools, and garages are shared. Also check whether rentals run for a weekend or a whole week, whether you must pay utility bills, and whether bed linen is covered by the rental agreement. Finally, check whether your possessions are covered by the lessee's house insurance policy in case of theft.

Useful address

There's a company backed by the government called the Fédération Nationale des Gîtes de France (59 rue St-Lazare, 75439 Paris, tel: 01 49 70 75 75, info@gites-de-france.fr, www.gites-de-france.fr), which produces a number of publications covering France's 55,000 holiday homes and bed and breakfast establishments. Visitors to Bordeaux should ask for details on Aquitaine, the Gironde and/or the southwest.

Staying in a château

Perhaps surprisingly, given its wealth of châteaux, Bordeaux has been slower than other French regions to offer château holidays, perhaps because Bordeaux châteaux tend to be working vineyards. Financial pressures like falling sales, inheritance tax, and massive bills for upkeep, however, mean there are more opportunities for those seeking the authentic château experience.

For further details contact Château-Accueil (25 rue Jean Giraudoux, 75116 Paris, tel: 01 53 67 74 00, www. chateau-accueil.com, rp@chateauxcountry).

Camping and caravanning

Camping in the Bordeaux region can offer the greatest-value accommodation, especially if you book at least six months ahead for July and August, and if you then get lucky with the weather. Expect four people in a car to pay what a couple would in a bed and breakfast.

Campsites in France are rated with stars, with four-star sites offering the most in terms of facilities. The bulk of the Bordeaux

ABOVE *A café in Bordeaux's city centre. People-watching is a national pastime.*

RIGHT *A specially made vineyard tractor that straddles the rows of vines.*

region's campsites are found along the Atlantic coast and thus are the best part of an hour away from the Left Bank vineyards of the Médoc and Graves. Pitching tents on private land (*camping sauvage*) is unwise, not just because you will be prosecuted. You may end up getting shot, by accident, by hunters who have the right to roam over large parts of the French countryside, including private land.

Useful address

For information about campsites, contact Fédération Française de Camping et Caravaning (78 rue de Rivoli, 75004 Paris, tel: 01 42 72 84 08, info@ffcc.fr, www.ffcc.fr). This produces a number of guides to French campsites, or ask at tourist offices for recommendations.

Hotels

The hotel rating system in France is similar to that for campsites – a one- to four-star system based on the facilities offered and not on overall quality: the size of bedrooms, room service, telephone and internet access, and so on. The most luxurious four-star hotels are usually called four-star deluxe, with three stars described as first class, two stars as standard, and one star as budget. "HT" hotels have not been rated.

Family run establishments which are members of the Logis de France group (www.logis-de-france.fr) tend to offer better value than the more impersonal but grand Relais & Châteaux (www.relaischateaux.com) not just in terms of money, but in terms of "the France experience", too.

And remember: don't try to stay at the Hôtel de Ville, as this is the French for "town hall".

Youth hostels

For youth hostels contact the French Youth Hostels Federation (FUAJ, FUAJ Centre National, 27 rue Pajol, 75018 Paris, tel: 01 44 89 87 27, centre-national@fuaj.org, www.fuaj.org). To stay in a French youth hostel (*une auberge de jeunesse*) you'll need to be a member of the FUAJ.

You can obtain a membership card from your national association (*see* the International Youth Hostel website: www.hihostels.com) or buy a Welcome Stamp for the first six nights in France. You will then be entitled to full membership for a year and have access to hostels worldwide.

The winemakers

B ordeaux is no different from any other wine region in that the people who make the wine are either the owners or are paid employees. As a generalization, the Left Bank is dominated by professional winemakers, while on the Right Bank it tends to be the owner getting his or her hands dirty come the harvest. This simply reflects the fact that many of Bordeaux's blue-chip châteaux on the Left Bank are now owned by companies rather than individuals or families. The reason for this is France's punitive inheritance laws.

How to be a winemaker

Professional winemakers often study at Bordeaux University, where the oenology faculty is among the best in the world (351, cours de la Libération, 33400 Talence, www. u-bordeaux2.fr) in Bordeaux's city suburbs. It was founded in 1880 by Ulysse Gayon, a former pupil of Louis Pasteur, the French scientist who was the first to work out that yeast was responsible for the process of fermentation.

Gayon discovered how copper sulphate spray protected vines from downy mildew; a vital discovery in Bordeaux's damp climate, where mildew thrives. Today, copper sulphate solution is mixed with lime, to neutralize its acidity, and sprayed on as "Bordeaux mixture". It is used across the world: if you see bright

ABOVE *Vine nurseries
(pepinières) are big business
around Civrac-sur-Dordogne
in Entre-Deux-Mers.*

RIGHT *Wooden basket presses
are the slowest way of pressing
grapes, but potentially give the
best quality juice.*

blue stains on posts in a vineyard, you'll know Bordeaux mixture has been used.

The current head of the oenology faculty is Yves Glories. He has researched how best to extract colour and flavour from the skins of red grapes. Glories says that if grapes are picked perfectly ripe, colour, and flavour are at their peak, but that the period of perfect ripeness lasts just four hours.

One of the faculty's finest minds for white wine is Denis Dubourdieu, owner of Château Reynon in the Premières Côtes (*see p.128*). He has discovered that soaking the juice with the skins for a few hours before pressing gives white wines more aroma and flavour. The technique is called "skin contact".

The alternative way

If Bordeaux University's faculty of oenology is mainly concerned with winemaking, Bordeaux also has wine-growing colleges (*lycées viticoles*) in Blanquefort and Montagne St-Emilion where vineyard management can be studied.

Pupils are normally sent off to work at affiliated vineyards such as Château La Tour Blanche in Bommes in Sauternes and Château Dillon in Blanquefort in the Haut-Médoc.

Professional crossover

It used to be that vineyard managers and winemakers worked independently of each other, but modern thinking favours as much crossover as possible between the two disciplines. The favoured adages are "great wine is made in the vineyard, not the winery" and "you can make a poor wine from great grapes but you'll never make a great wine from poor grapes".

The importance of the blender

This is the key job in Bordeaux. Almost all the reds, and most whites, are blends of more than one grape variety. The reason is that in Bordeaux blends work best. A 100 per cent Cabernet Sauvignon here would be intense but would need rounding out: Cabernet can be a little lean on its own. *See p.21* for what the different grapes bring to the blend.

Bordeaux-lovers pay great attention to the percentages of each grape in the blends of their favourite châteaux, as each vintage the blends will subtly change.

How Bordeaux makes wine

Wine is simply the mid-point between grape juice and vinegar. Wine is made when the sugars in grape juice are turned into alcohol by the action of yeast. But leave a bottle of wine unstoppered and bacteria will turn it to vinegar or *vin aigre* – literally, "sour wine".

Going wild

Fermentation can be started either by the wild yeasts present in the air or in the bloom on the grape-skins, or by adding commercially produced dried yeasts.

After the yeasts have fermented the sugar to alcohol they die and sink to the bottom, forming a sludge called lees. If the grapes were healthy at harvest-time, the wine can be left on the lees for a few days, weeks or even months. This will make the wine's flavours extra-rich. But if the grapes were unhealthy, the lees will make the wine smell dirty, and the wine must be drawn off (racked) into clean tanks as quickly as possible.

Dry white wine

The grapes are pressed and the juice collected in either tanks or oak barrels for fermentation. Pips and skins are discarded. White fermentations usually last from several days to a couple of weeks. The temperature is normally controlled to between 14–20°C (57–68°F). Any hotter, and the wines would lose their delicacy.

Basic dry white Bordeaux is best drunk within a couple of years of the harvest. To keep it as fresh as possible it is bottled within six months. More expensive versions, wholly or partly fermented in oak barrels, will be bottled within eighteen months of the harvest. The best can age for a decade or more.

Most white winemakers in Bordeaux prefer not to allow the secondary fermentation called the malolactic to occur. The malolactic turns appley tasting malic acid into buttery-tasting lactic acid.

Sparkling wines

This is Crémant de Bordeaux, which can be white, pink or red. Any of the Bordeaux red or white grapes can be used.

Sparkling Bordeaux is made in the same way as Champagne. A dry white wine is made in the normal way (even the clear juice of red grapes can be used), and then bottled with a little added yeast and sugar. The yeasts create a second alcoholic fermentation in the sealed bottle. As the carbon dioxide created by the yeast cannot escape, it stays in the wine under pressure. The lees are allowed to settle in the neck of the bottle by turning it gradually upside-down over a period of weeks. Then the bottle neck is frozen and the plug of ice and lees removed. The bottle is immediately topped up with more fizzy wine and corked ready for sale.

Sweet white wines

The grapes are usually picked late, to allow them to rot nobly on the vine: harvest often doesn't take place until mid-October, and even on into November.

In theory, if all the sugar present in these grapes was fermented the wine would contain around nineteen to twenty-one degrees of alcohol. Instead, what happens is that the yeasts give up when the alcohol level becomes too high for them, at around 13.5 degrees. This leaves lots of unfermented or residual sugar. It is this which gives late-picked wines their intense sweetness.

Red wines

The grape juice is clear in colour: the colour of red wines comes from the skins. The juice is therefore fermented with the skins, and the alcohol acts as a solvent, leeching colour and tannins into the wine. Tannins help red Bordeaux to age for many years, and in the case of the best wines, many decades.

After picking, the grapes are separated from the stems. Then the grapes are crushed. The mush of juice, pips, and skins is then pumped into the fermenting vats. Most Bordeaux winemakers feel leaving the stems in the tanks would create unwanted vegetal flavours.

For red wine to get its colour and tannin, the increasingly alcoholic juice must be in contact with the skins. So juice is pumped from the bottom of the tank over the skins at the top. This is called, not surprisingly, pumping-over (*remontage* in French), and it usually happens every morning and evening.

Colour extraction is encouraged by heat, so red wine tanks are allowed to ferment at 26–35°C (79–95°F). Fermentation is usually over within a week or two. Afterwards, the young wine is left in contact with the skins for several more days or weeks to ensure maximum flavour and colour are extracted.

After tasting each tank daily, the winemaker will decide when the wine can be run off the skins into tanks or oak barrels. The skins are then pressed. This press wine, if of good quality, can be blended in small percentages into the main wine for extra structure.

LEFT *Vines grown low to the ground are common in parts of Bordeaux.*

BELOW *Bending barrel staves over a fire.*

Pink wines and *clairets*

Pink wine is made in the same way as red wine, but because only a moderate amount of colour is needed for pink wine the fermenting wine is drawn off the skins after only a few hours of fermentation. Deeper-coloured pink wines or *clairets* will be drawn off after slightly longer. The wine is then fermented in the same way as white wine.

Barrels and tanks

The barrel size associated with Bordeaux is the barrique, which holds 225 litres, or 300 bottles. Traditionally wine is traded by Bordeaux merchants by the *tonneau* – 900 litres or four barriques' worth – rather than by the bottle.

If you want to see how barrels are made it is worth taking a trip to the family owned Lasserre barrelmakers, Tonnellerie Lasserre, in Vertheuil in St-Estèphe (rue du Bayle, 33180 Vertheuil, tel: 05 56 41 98 03, www.tonnellerielasserre.com, contact@tonn ellerielasserre.com). Tours take around half an hour and a small fee is payable.

Visiting producers and winery etiquette

Visiting a Bordeaux château is a little more formal than visiting a winery in California or a small grower in Burgundy, for example. For the Bordelais wine is first and foremost a business. It also pays to look tidy. Bordeaux is quite a formal place, and men should wear a shirt rather than a T-shirt, especially at the top châteaux, although jeans are fine.

Shaken not stirred

When you arrive and depart it is quite normal in France to shake hands with your hosts. However, don't expect to start kissing people on both cheeks unless you have established a real friendship.

Bordeaux wineries are inundated with requests for visits, and punctuality is expected. So, ensure you arrive bang on time – not five minutes early or five minutes late. Distances between châteaux appear deceptively small on the map, so plan well ahead when booking appointments. Tell your potential host when booking which other châteaux you are visiting locally. They can tell you whether your timings are realistic.

Most visits take thirty minutes to an hour. Whereas, in California or Burgundy you'll taste up to half a dozen wines, in the Médoc, St-Emilion or Pomerol you might be offered just one wine, usually the latest vintage. Visits tend to last longer on the Right Bank, and at the less famous, often family owned estates.

Practise spitting

If tasting from bottle in a tasting room, a spittoon will usually be provided for you to empty your glass or spit the wine. Don't be embarassed about spitting, or about asking for a napkin with which to wipe your mouth if things get messy. Even professional tasters have been known to get it wrong and dribble sometimes.

It is quite normal to spit wine out on the floor, or the drainage gutter under the lines of tanks or barrels, unless a spittoon has been provided. When tasting the most expensive wines from barrel allow the host to tip the remains of your glass back into the barrel if need be.

Rinsing your glass with a little wine first to get rid of any musty smells, or those picked up from drying cloths, is perfectly acceptable. It shows

RIGHT *Signs for châteaux are generally plentiful – just watch out for local drivers.*

BELOW *As Bordeaux's sweetest whites age, their colour changes from bright golden to darker caramel.*

your host that you are serious and you want to see the wine at its best. The French verb for wine rinsing like this is *"aviner"*, to be distinguished from *"aviné"*, which means "drunken".

When tasting in the winery you will taste from tank or barrel, and this will probably not be the final blend, so ask the producer what you are tasting.

What you are given to taste can also depend on the time of year. During harvest you will be offered a taste of the grape juice drawn straight from the press – for white whites – or the grape crusher – for reds. It will look a bit murky but will taste deliciously sweet.

Don't be afraid of tasting fermenting wines. They'll be a bit fizzy – carbon dioxide is given off by the yeast – but the fruit flavours are usually very pronounced.

In the weeks after the end of harvest you will be offered a taste of each grape variety as it sits in tank, which is a great way of learning the differences. Wines from the different varieties are usually blended together in spring, so only then will you be offered a taste of the new blends.

Ask for a price list and write tasting notes on it as you go. This provides a useful souvenir of your visit and will help you work out your favourite styles of wine. It will also show your host you are a wine-lover, not a time-wasting tourist.

And lastly, if you see a château you like the look of but you haven't made an appointment, you stand absolutely zero chance of being welcomed between midday and 2pm, for lunch in France is a religion. So always book ahead to avoid any possibility of disappointment.

DAYS TO AVOID – FRENCH PUBLIC HOLIDAYS (*FERIES*)

JANUARY: 1 Le Jour de l'An.
MARCH/APRIL: Easter Monday, Paques.
MAY: 1 La Fête du Travail 8 La Fête de la Libération.
MAY/JUNE: Ascension Day, L'Ascension; **Pentecost/ Whit Monday**, La Pentecôte, both dates depending on the date of Easter.
JULY: 14 La Fête Nationale.
AUGUST: 15 The Assumption, L'Assomption de la Vierge.
NOVEMBER: 1 All Saints, Toussaint; 11 La Fête de la Victoire 1918.
DECEMBER: 25 Noël.

Neither **Good Friday** nor **December 26** are public holidays. Many châteaux close between **August 1–15**. In **September**, there is a Les Journées de la Patrimoine (National Heritage Weekend) of open doors at relevant sites, such as Château La Brède, Graves (*see* p.89).

Time out from wine

Without wine, Bordeaux would be nothing and, some would say, without Bordeaux wine wouldn't be anything either. If you want to find a vine-free space, go walking in the Landes forests, catch a boat out to sea, or try one of these.

Climb a dune

The Dune du Pyla is the highest sand dune in Europe. At 120m (394 feet) high, and 3km (1.9 miles) in length, it dominates the entrance to the Basin d'Arcachon, less than one hour's drive due west of Bordeaux city (take the toll-free N250 or the toll-paying A6, leaving at junction 22 for the A660). The sand is eating into the pine forests to the east at a rate of 4m (13 feet) per year, and has already consumed a hotel, but the Bassin is a great spot for oysters, bathing on soft, white, sandy beaches, and windsurfing. Campers should try Pyla Camping (33115 Pyla-sur-Mer, tel: 05 56 22 74 56, pylacamping@free.fr). Local bus services run from Arcachon centre to the dune 8km (5 miles) away.

BELOW AND RIGHT *French street markets remain a great source of fresh produce, and prices often undercut the supermarkets.*

Watch top sporting action

Bordeaux's football club (Football Club des Girondins de Bordeaux, contact@girondins.com, www.girondins.com) has won the French league title five times – the last time in 1999. The home colours are similar to that of the French national side: navy blue shirts and white shorts. The club is owned by businessman and Listrac winemaker, Jean-Luis Triaud.

The 35,000-seater stadium was called Parque Lescure until 2001 when it was renamed Stade Jacques Chaban-Delmas. It is located 2km (1 mile) from Bordeaux town centre at 347 Boulevard Wilson, Place Johnston, 33000 Bordeaux. For tickets call 0892 68 34 33; ask for *virage sud* or *virage nord* to be behind the goals (mainly uncovered) or the

tribune de face latérale/centrale to be seated in the middle and in a covered area.

Bordeaux's local rugby club, the CABBG (Club Athlétique Bordeaux Bègles Gironde) is based at 25 rue Delphin Loche (33130 Bègles, tel: 05 56 85 94 01, www.cabbg.fr, contact@cabbg.fr) and run on an amateur basis (a recent move to professional status was problematic). From the centre of Bordeaux take the boulevards (inner ring road) to the Barrière de Bègles; follow signs to Bègles centre, then Stade A Moga.

Visit Cognac and Armagnac

Fed up with wine, but still need a drink? Luckily, Bordeaux is sandwiched between the world's two greatest brandy regions: Cognac to the north and Armagnac to the south. Armagnac is usually distilled once compared with Cognac's twice, and has a more fiery, intense character. Armagnac is reached by taking the A62, direction Toulouse, leaving at exit 7 (Agen) for the D931 to Condom, Armagnac's main town. Journey time is two-hours-plus.

Go to the opera

Operatic, choral, and dance events take place either at Bordeaux's opera house in the magnificent late-eighteenth-century Grand Théâtre on the Place de la Comédie, or are staged at other venues in the city such as Le Palais des Sports, on the Place de la Ferme de Richemont. (Opéra National de Bordeaux, Place de la Comédie, 33000 Bordeaux, tel: 05 56 00 85 95, courrier@opera-bordeaux.com, www.opera-bordeaux.com.) There are also guided tours of the theatre.

LOCAL INFORMATION

TOURIST OFFICES: Armagnac
Place Bossuet
32100 Condom
Tel: 05.62.28.00.80
otsi@condom.org

Cognac
16 rue du 14 Juillet
11600 Cognac
Tel: 05 45 82 10 71
www.ville-cognac.fr
office.tourisme.cognac@
wanadoo.fr

Archachon
Esplanade Georges
Pompidou, 33311 Arcachon
Tel: 05 57 52 97 97
www.arcachon.com
**This office can help with
windsurfing and other
watery activities.**

How to get your wine home

Y ou can't buy wine direct from the most elite châteaux as it is all sold on the internal Bordeaux market (*see* p.12). However, from less grand estates you can buy wine in bulk (*en vrac*) direct from the tank or barrel, in bottle (*par bouteille*) or by the twelve-bottle case (*par caisse*).

The tax question

You must pay French tax or duty if you intend to drink the wine in France — if you have a holiday home there, for example. Such wine is sold "TTC" or *toutes taxes comprises* and carries the symbol of the French republic on the capsule covering the cork.

If the wine is leaving France ask for the duty-free (*hors taxe*) price (*tarif*) but keep your receipt (*le reçu*) and travel documents with you at all times.

Bringing wine home

You don't need to be a genius to work out that wine is fragile, heavy, and unwieldy. I have lost count of the times I have seen suitcases sodden by red wines that have got crushed in transit. And airlines are getting increasingly strict about the weight allowances for carry-on luggage.

The baggage allowance for the cross-Channel train service Eurostar (tel: 08705 186186) is two large items and one small item per person. If you can tape a couple of wine boxes together this will count as one item.

Post-haste

RIGHT *Haut-Brion is one of the few great vineyards to be located in a city suburb.*

BELOW *Wine shops in Bordeaux can be like jewellers, so don't touch unless you can pay for what you drop.*

Posting your wine home is another option, if you can find the right way of packaging it — usually a polystyrene single-bottle tube set in a cardboard sheath. Some châteaux might have these for sale — but don't bank on it.

Posting wine home would only make financial sense if the wine was fairly to very expensive — but you would need to insure it as well as pay the high postage costs. You can't post wine to the USA, where each state has its own rules on the importation of alcohol, and the federal

government has increasingly stringent restrictions on wine. It is classed as a food product, so its label must conform to the the USA's byzantine, absurd, and protectionist labelling laws.

Fill your boots

Transporting wine within the European Union is fairly straightforward if it is for personal consumption and not re-sale once it has crossed a border.

Cross-channel "booze cruisers" have complained of persecution by the UK customs service, Her Majesty's Customs and Excise, so know your rights – and their rules. For advice on allowances, contact HM Customs and Excise National Advice Service (tel: 0845 010 9000, www.hmce.gov.uk).

The rules in brief

Any alcohol or tobacco you bring in must be for your own use. You can take ninety litres of wine into the UK, which equates to ten cases of twelve 75cl bottles. This is enough, the UK government says, for one person to drink up to half a litre of wine per day for six months!

If you wish to bring in more than this amount, expect to prove that either you are a very heavy drinker (via a doctor's note) or that the wine is for a party or a wedding.

If Customs think that the goods are for a commercial purpose they may seize them and any vehicle used to transport them, and you may not have them returned to you.

If you are caught smuggling or selling alcohol this may be seized, and for a serious offence you could get up to seven years in prison.

FURTHER OPTIONS FOR THE UK

If you strike up a good relationship with a particular grower, you could **import their wine direct**. You will need to **organize a carrier**, one who will pay the duty on wine, you having paid the carrier upfront.

You would **pay the ex-cellars price** for the wine at the château, the carrier's costs and the duty. You will also have to **find space to store the wine** once it arrives in the UK.

If it goes to **a bonded warehouse** you don't have to pay the duty in advance, but will pay storage and administation charges each time you want to "uplift" wine, and duty on a piecemeal basis. You will be classed as what is called **an Occasional Importer**.

Discovering
Vineyards in
Bordeaux

Lesparre-Médoc and northern Médoc

The northern part of the Médoc peninsula begins north of St-Seurin-de-Cadourne (*see* St-Estèphe map p.51). Its old name was Bas-Médoc or Lower Médoc, because it lies further downstream than the Haut-Médoc. It can seem the most desolate place in Bordeaux, especially in winter, when the lowness of the sun in the sky accentuates a flat and largely featureless landscape. Vineyards are less frequent here than further south, the villages are smaller and less obviously touristy, and the only sounds you are likely to hear are the wind and the lowing of cows, for apart from forestry and wine, cattle rearing is the main agricultural activity.

The Dutch influence

Any land here not given to agriculture of one form or another is generally low-lying marsh, so bear that in mind if you pull your car to the side of the road to check the map or enjoy an impromptu picnic. This part of the Médoc was drained by Dutch engineers who, from the seventeenth century onwards, built a system of dykes. The land was planted with vines and corn, and windmills like the restored one in Blaignan (*see* Château Tour Haut-Caussan p.45) came to dominate the landscape.

The name of the hamlet of By is said to be Dutch in origin, and if you flick through the pages of the local telephone book, you'll see many Dutch-sounding names, often descendants of the original engineers. And don't be surprised to find some restaurants and guest-houses serving food laden with rich, creamy, Flemish-style sauces.

Vine frenzy

In the nineteenth century, as Bordeaux wines became ever more popular, vineyard planting in the Médoc reached a frenzy. London wine and spirits merchants the Gilbey brothers bought Château Loudenne (*see* p.45) and turned it into a major cellar complex, from where casks could be loaded via a small railway onto boats for the sea-voyage to the UK.

BELOW *Sometimes it's worth going to a restaurant just for the exterior.*

ABOVE *Camping in the Médoc is as popular with locals as it is with tourists. Make sure you book ahead.*

The Gilbeys even built a little dock to which barges could tie up to be loaded. It was still in use after World War II.

Tourist-free

The great thing about visiting this part of the Médoc today is that it is comparatively free of tourists, and château visits can be leisurely affairs. Tourists travelling up from Bordeaux tend to get seduced by the famous classed-growth wineries in the Haut-Médoc's flagship areas of Margaux, St-Julien, Pauillac, and St-Estèphe, and ignore the Médoc. The only thing you need to bear in mind is distances between châteaux here tend to be greater than further south, and it is much easier to get lost as there are so few obvious landmarks.

Bargain-hunting

Apart from the southern Graves, south of Bordeaux city, the Médoc is the best place on the Left Bank for red wine bargains. Médoc wines are generally less complex-tasting than their counterparts from the Haut-Médoc, but have the advantage of maturing after only a few years, rather than needing a decade or more.

One reason is that the soil has more clay, which suits the early ripening and early maturing Merlot grape, which can account for fifty per cent of a typical blend. Cabernet Sauvignon and Cabernet Franc usually make up the remainder.

If you don't manage to make appointments at the châteaux specifically recommended in these pages, you can try your luck at estates in what are considered the better wine-producing villages here, such as Bégadan, Ordonnac, Potensac, St-Christoly, St-Germain-d'Esteuil, and St-Yzans.

The best Médoc reds are characterised by their moderate level of alcohol, with 12–12.5 degrees usual compared to 13 degrees or more in some St-Emilion and Pomerol reds, and moreish fruit, usually hidden behind the tannin if the wines are very young. One tip is to serve younger wines a bit above room temperature to make them more accessible. Serious wine-lovers steer clear of the cheapest Médocs, which can taste thin and mean, and opt instead for producers like Tour Haut-Caussan and Les Ormes-Sorbet (see p.45) who produce wines of near-classed-growth quality for a fraction of the price.

LOCAL INFORMATION

**Office de Tourisme
de Lesparre**
place du Docteur
Lapeyrade
33340 Lesparre-Médoc
Tel: 05 56 41 21 96
www.tourisme.fr/tourist-
office/lesparre-
medoc.htm

Getting there

By car, from Bordeaux take the N215 to Lesparre (around one hour) or the slower D2 via Pauillac to St-Yzans (around ninety minutes). Using public transport, Lesparre is seventy-five minutes by train from Gare St-Jean in Bordeaux. Alternatively you can take CITRAM Aquitaine buses from place des Quinconces in Bordeaux centre, destination Lesparre, and connect to local services from there.

Travelling around

There are two possible itineraries for this region.

Route one: begins in St-Yzans-de-Médoc and takes you to Couquèques, St-Christoly, and Port-de-By, then to Villeneueve, Valeyrac, Bégadan, Blaignan (Caussan), Ordonnac, St-Germain d'Esteuil, and back to either Lesparre or St-Estephe. The route length is 20–25km (12–15 miles).

Route two: will take you from Lesparre through Gaillan-en-Médoc, Vensac, Jau, Dignac, Loirac, and Queyrac. This route covers 40km (25 miles).

Lesparre-Médoc: route one
Take half a day for classy châteaux and great river views

Lesparre-Médoc: route two
Allow the best part of a day

ST VIVIEN-DE-MÉDOC

la Brasserie

Jau

Dignac

Port de Goulée

Noaillac

Vensac

Valeyrac

Loirac

Villeneuve

D103

la Verdasse

D201

D2

Girond e

Port-de-By

Courbian

By

D3

D102

Canissac

Queyrac

D103

Bégadan

St-Christoly-Médoc

Couquèques

Civrac-en-Médoc

D103 D103

Queyzans

Prignac-en-Médoc

Gaillan-en-Médoc

D201   D3

Caussan

Moulin de Courrian

St-Yzans-de-Médoc

D2

Lafon

D4

Ordonnac

St Estèphe

LESPARRE-MÉDOC

Plautignan

Chenal de la Maréchale

D204

D203

St Estèphe

St-Germain-d'Esteuil

N215

D4

Artiguillon

N215

0   2 Km
0   2 miles

ABOVE *The Pointe de Grave is where the Gironde estuary meets the Atlantic.*

RIGHT *Low-trained, tightly spaced vines are typical of the Médoc vineyards.*

Route one: in the pink

Travel from the Haut-Médoc commune of St-Seurin-de-Cadourne (*see* St-Estèphe, p.49), and take the D2 north into the Médoc and St-Yzans-de-Médoc to visit the pink-painted Château Loudenne overlooking the Gironde (*see right*).

This nineteenth-century château with museum was once owned by the Gilbeys of gin fame. Meals are available if you order in advance. There is a fee for tasting, but the cost is reduced for groups of eight or more. Follow signs to Château Loudenne *chais* for visits. Loudenne's vineyard is claimed to be the highest in this part of the Médoc, at all of 16m (53 feet) above sea level.

Sea shells of Couquèques

Couquèques takes its name from layers of fossilized sea-shells in its limestone soils, said to give the local red wines their aroma and elegance. From the centre of St-Yzans take the D103 to Château les Ormes-Sorbet in Couquéques (*see right*).

Owned by the Boivert family since 1620, this has been consistently one of the best Médoc estates. Visits here are by appointment only.

From Couquèques, stay on the D103, in the direction of St-Christoly-Médoc, where notable local wine producers include Château La Tour-St-Bonnet (tel: 05 56 41 53 03) and

Château Rollan-de-By (tel: 05 56 41 58 59, rollan-de-by@wanadoo.fr). There is a small wine museum at Rollan-de-By showing old cooperage equipment, plus a modern winery with wide stainless steel vats for easier extraction of colour from red grapes: the wide top gives a greater surface area of skins.

Worth the climb

At St-Christoly-Médoc, join the D2 north to the Port-de-By and the eastern part of Bégadan where, by taking a left onto the D3, one finds Château La Tour-de-By which affords a superb view of the Gironde (see right). The tower here dates from 1825 and was a lighthouse beacon. Visitors can climb it and then enjoy a free tasting. The château is open daily, except on Bastille Day (July 14), the feast of the Assumption (August 15), and during harvest.

Return to the D2 and head to Valeyrac, where there is a charming harbour for pleasure-craft, the Porte de Goulée. Leading estates here include Château Sipian (tel: 05 56 41 56 05) which especially welcomes group visits, and Château Bellegrave (tel: 05 56 41 53 83), which has good visitor facilities, including a dedicated tasting room and a small museum of old vineyard tools.

CHATEAUX IN NORTHERN MEDOC
. . . .
Château Le Bernadot
Gaudin
33590 Vensac
Tel: 05 56 09 57 94 *(D5)*

Château Loudenne
33340 St-Yzans-de-Médoc
Tel: 05 56 73 17 80 *(B1)*
chateau-loudenne@wanadoo.fr

Château Les Ormes-Sorbet
33340 Couquèques
Tel: 05 56 41 53 78 *(B2)*
ormes.sorbet@wanadoo.fr

Château Preuillac
33340 Lesparre
Tel: 05 56 09 00 29 *(A2)*

Château la Tour-de-By
33340 Bégadan
Tel: 05 56 41 50 03 *(C2)*
la.tour.de.by@wanadoo.fr

Château Tour-Haut-Caussan
33340 Blaignan
Tel: 05 56 09 06 26/
05 56 09 00 77 *(B2)*

PRICES: moderate to expensive

Around Bégadan

From Valeyrac head to the centre of Bégadan via either the D103E through the hamlet of la Verdasse, or the D201 to the north through the hamlet of Sipian. South of Bégadan are Château Plagnac (tel: 05 56 31 44 44) and Vieux Château Landon (chateau.landon@wanadoo.fr).

To the north is Château Patache-d'Aux (tel: 05 56 41 50 18, info@domaines-lapalu.com) which stands on a former stagecoach stop.

Before the 1789 Revolution the then owners, the d'Aux family, ran the stagecoach service, a fact commemorated both on Patache-d'Aux's label and in the name of its second wine, called Relais de Patache.

From Bégadan take the D3, direction Lesparre, as far as Civrac-en-Médoc, taking signs to the hamlet of Caussan for Château Tour Haut-Caussan (see right). Here owner Philippe Courrian has restored the sails of a windmill

WHERE TO STAY

BED AND BREAKFAST:
**Château Rousseau
de Sipian**
rue du Port de Goulée,
33340 Valeyrac
Tel: 05 56 41 54 92
rousseaudesipian@aol.com
A Renaissance-style
château set in its own
park and offering bed
and breakfast, by prior
reservation only.
English spoken.

La Caleche
2 route de la Landeuille
33340 Bégadan
Tel: 05 56 41 35 49
Bed and breakfast in a
typical Médoc stone
house. Three rooms
available. Closed in
February.

HOTELS: **Hotel des Vieux
Acacias**
33340 Queyrac
Tel: 05 56 59 80 63
tourhotel@vieuxacacias.com
This hotel has comfortable
rooms and apartments
and is just ten minutes'
drive from the Atlantic
beaches.

CAMPING: **Camping Les
Acacias**
44 route de St Vivien
33590 Vensac
Tel: 05 56 09 58 81
les.Acacias.en.medoc
@wanadoo.fr
Offers camping,
swimming pool,
bar-restaurant,
mini-golf, mobile home
rental, solarium and
washing machine/
drying facilities.

built in 1734, called the Moulin de Courrian (see picture p.7),
which is located in one of his vine parcels. The château
produces serious, fragrant reds; visits by appointment only.

Raise the drawbridge
From Caussan, head west along the D203 Lesparre-St-Seurin-
de-Cadourne road to rejoin the N215 to Bordeaux south of
Lesparre. On the way you will pass Château Preuillac and its
wine school (see p.48) and the nearby Château Chantelys in
Lafon, run with organic priciples by Christine Braquessac-
Courrian (tel: 05 56 09 02 78).

If you want to go back to Bordeaux on the slower D2
from Caussan, take the D203 to St-Seurin-de-Cadourne and
turn right after less than 3km (2 miles) at Plautignan for
Château Castéra (www.chateau-castera.fr), a castle with a
drawbridge that was raised to foil the Black Prince, son of
King Edward III of England, who in the fourteenth century was
laying siege to it.

Route two: an English stronghold
Lesparre-Médoc, to give it its full title, is the northern Médoc's
major population centre, with around 5,000 inhabitants. It
lies on the N215 Bordeaux-Le Verdon road, 68km (43 miles)
from Bordeaux. Lesparre was a stronghold of the English
during the Hundred Years' War
(1337–1453), a period evoked by the
square-framed Tour de l'Honneur on the
outskirts of the town, which houses a
museum. Details from the Lesparre tourist
office (see p.42).

International flavour
Head north from Lesparre on the N215
through Gaillan-en-Médoc up to
Vensac, 12km (8 miles) away. Follow
signs just north of the town at Gaudin to
Château Le Bernadot (see p.45). This
small vineyard is run by Scotsman John
Robertson and his Japanese wife Fujiko.
It produces good value, floral-scented
reds. A prior appointment is necessary.

At this point you can continue up the
N215 for St-Vivien-de-Médoc, but the
vineyards peter out at Talais. The N215
continues to Soulac-sur-Mer (see p.48)
and Le Verdon, where you can catch
the ferry to Royan (see "Tip for a quick
trip", p.25). Otherhwise, from Château Le

Bernadot head east back across the N215 and the low-lying marshland to Jau, Dignac, and Loirac – three small communes amalgamated administratively into one. From Dignac you can see the lighthouse, *le phare de Richard*, on the Gironde estuary.

Visitor-friendly estates here include Château Noaillac in Noillac (tel: 05 56 09 52 20, noaillac@noaillac.com), and Château Laulan-Ducos in Laulan (tel: 05 56 09 42 37, www.laulanducos.com), both west of Loirac. Take the D103E from Loirac to Queyrac, where Château Carcannieux (tel: 05 56 59 84 23) has a gleaming winery with an impressive semi-underground barrel cellar. From Queyrac the D102 takes you back to the N215 and south through Lesparre to Bordeaux.

To the lighthouse

The old Cardouan lighthouse (*le phare de Cardouan*) was built from 1584 and still guards where the Gironde and the Atlantic ocean meet northwest of Le Verdon and the Pointe de Grave. It is a national historic monument. Boat trips run from June to September. Contact the Le Verdon tourist office (tel: 05 56 09 60 19, www.littoral33.com).

Back to nature

Montalivet-les-Bains town and beach (www.montalivetinfo.com) have been a naturist and nudist community since 1953, with

BELOW *Sand dunes like Arcachon's Dune du Pyla might engulf the Médoc but for the Landes forests which act as a break on its eastward progress.*

RIGHT *Small canals were dug from the seventeenth century by Dutch engineers to drain the Médoc and make it suitable for vine-growing.*

most visitors being family groups. If you want to visit, leave your clothes – and your camera – in the car. The Euronat naturist camp in nearby Grayan-l'Hôpital to the north (tel: 05 56 09 33 33, info@ euronat.fr) has direct access to the beach. It is the largest naturist camp in Europe.

WHERE TO EAT

Restaurant des Pins
33780 Amelie-sur-Mer
Tel: 05 56 73 27 27
hotel.pin@wanadoo.fr
Hotel/restaurant 100m (328 feet) from the beach 5km (3 miles) south of Soulac on the D101E.

Restaurant la Maison du Douanier
2 route de By, Port de St-Christoly-de-Médoc, 33340 St-Christoly-de-Médoc
Tel: 05 56 41 35 25
Traditional dishes cooked in a modern style. Overlooks the Gironde. Closed Tuesdays and January 5 to February 11.

Château Lagauya
route de Verdon
33340 Gaillan-en-Médoc
Tel: 05 56 41 26 83
Former wine château 3km (1.8 miles) north of Lesparre, surrounded by vines with good menu featuring lobster, foie gras de canard, and so on. Comfortable rooms, too.

Tasting courses

Château Preuillac is a working château with its own wine school, where visitors can learn about tasting, the region, and the basics of winemaking. Most courses are in English and are run by a British Master of Wine, Richard Bampfield. The school encourages guests to get their hands dirty in the vineyard during their stay.

The great thing about the courses at Preuillac is that they are informal but very professional, making them reassuringly at odds with Bordeaux's sometimes stuffy image. Highly recommended. Accommodation is in double and twin rooms in the château, and a typical programme lasts three days, including visits to other estates both in the Mêdoc and St-Emilion. (*See* p.45.)

Seasonal highlights

Lesparre runs a wine festival at the beginning of August, while St-Yzans-de-Médoc has a Foire aux Sarments (Festival of Vine Prunings) in June. Details can be found at the tourist office in Lesparre (*see* p.42).

Northern Médoc wine facts

Wines from the northern part of the Médoc peninsula are reds labelled "Médoc". Around forty million bottles of Médoc are produced each year from 5,300ha of vines, or one third of the Médoc peninsula's total vineyard area.

There are 635 wine producers, 400 of which take their grapes to cooperatives (the cooperative movement in this part of Bordeaux remains strong). The rest of the producers bottle their own wines, but none of them are *grands crus classés*, or classed growths.

St-Estèphe

S t-Estèphe's fresh red wines are among Bordeaux's most underrated. Make your way to La Chapelle, the little port east of the village. It was around this port that St-Estephe's origins lay, and gave rise to the name of arguably its greatest estate, Calon-Ségur. Small boats called "*calones*" would cross the Gironde from here with timber hewn from the forests to the west. In the eighteenth century, Calon's owner, the Marquis de Ségur, who also owned Lafite and Latour in Pauillac proclaimed, "I make my wine at Lafite and Latour, but my heart is in Calon."

Long history

St-Estèphe's wine-growing tradition pre-dates the English rule of Bordeaux and was begun by thirteenth-century monks. Their priory is now Château Meyney's winery (tel: 05 56 31 44 44, château.meyney@free.fr). After the French finally expelled the English in 1453, St-Estèphe was where English ships had to tie up, pay tax, and be searched instead of at Bordeaux further up the Gironde. Like Meyney, most wineries in St-Estèphe and neighbouring Haut-Médoc communes like Cissac, Vertheuil, and St-Seurin-de-Cadourne are middle-class *crus bourgeois* rather than aristocratic *crus classés*. The wooded, clay-rich vineyards produce no-nonsense, ageworthy red wines offering good value when compared to those of Margaux, St-Julien, and Pauillac.

A good second

St-Estèphe has no First Growth winery, few really grand château buildings, and as much scrub and woodland as vineyard. Its relative isolation and distance from Bordeaux meant that red wine vineyards were developed here fully only from the nineteenth century, up to two centuries later than in Pauillac, St-Julien, and Margaux to the south. This partly explains why St-Estèphe was so poorly represented in the 1855 Classification. It boasts only two Second Growths (Cos d'Estournel and Montrose), one Third Growth (Calon-Ségur), one Fourth (Lafon-Rochet), and one Fifth (Cos Labory).

BELOW *Château Calon-Ségur's distinctive squat towers stand guard over the Gironde as it widens to meet the Atlantic.*

Classification aficionados view this with no sense of injustice. They say that St-Estèphe's soil has too much darkish clay to be considered top rank, and that the clay makes the wines thick and structured rather than giving them the smoothness that comes from more gravel-rich sites.

Going to ground

However, St-Estèphe's critics forget that what lies deeper underground is just as important in shaping a wine's overall character. Thick limestone underpins much of St-Estèphe, giving its wines intoxicating scents as well as great vivacity and an incredible capacity to age.

The greatest wines from Calon-Ségur, Montrose, Cos d'Estournel, and de Pez offer relative value for money compared to red wines of equivalent status from the Pauillac, Margaux, and St-Julien sub-regions, which tend to hog the limelight. Yet, the best St-Estèphes can be among the Haut-Médoc's most highly flavoured, highly charged clarets; just don't expect an easy ride if you plan to drink them within eight to fifteen years. Before then the wines can fool you into thinking the fruit is too firm and rather underflavoured, so learn to be patient.

The waiting game

For patience is what St-Estèphe is about. As the furthest north of the "big four" appellations in the Haut-Médoc, St-Estèphe experiences the most maritime climate. This gives it potentially the longest growing season, so wine-growers must wait (if they dare) until early October before finishing picking. This Atlantic-influenced climate enforces the kind of slow, steady ripening the two Cabernets need if they are to produce their greatest wines, although September squalls here can also cause an unripe note in cool, wet years.

Yet St-Estèphe's gravel soil is warm and deep enough (up to 10m/33 feet) for both its Cabernet Sauvignon and its less important but slightly earlier-ripening Cabernet Franc to develop their unique rich, dry insistency without becoming overripe; the clay provides Merlot with vibrant, inky-dark colours and scrumptious texture. The limestone subsoil rounds out the Cabernets' rougher edges and keeps the Merlot lively. It also gives St-Estèphe's red wines a vitalising, refreshing character that can send a shiver down your spine when you drink them cool from the barrel.

Getting there

St-Estèphe is forty-five minutes (50km/31 miles) by road from Bordeaux on the D2. If you want to go by rail, take a train from either Bordeaux St-Jean or Bordeaux St-Louis stations: the journey to Pauillac to the south or Lesparre to the northwest takes forty-five to eighty minutes.

LEFT Fridge-magnets are the most economical way of collecting Bordeaux's famous wine names.

Travelling around

Route one: takes in the famous names of St-Estèphe and begins in Cos, and takes you to Marbuzet, St-Estèphe, Pez, Leyssac, and back to Cos. The route could be driven in around forty minutes without a stop, and is approximately 13km (8 miles) long.

Route two: will take you around the backwoods chateaux of the Haut-Médoc, starting in Pauillac and going through Cos, Blagnac, Cissac-Médoc, Vertheuil, Pez, St-Corbian, and finishing in St-Seurin-de-Cadourne. This would take a good hour to drive without a stop, and is approximately 24km (15 miles) long.

The famous names

The leading châteaux are all easily accessible off the main road leading north from Pauillac to St-Estèphe village (*see route one*). St-Estèphe's two Second Growths lie within 2km

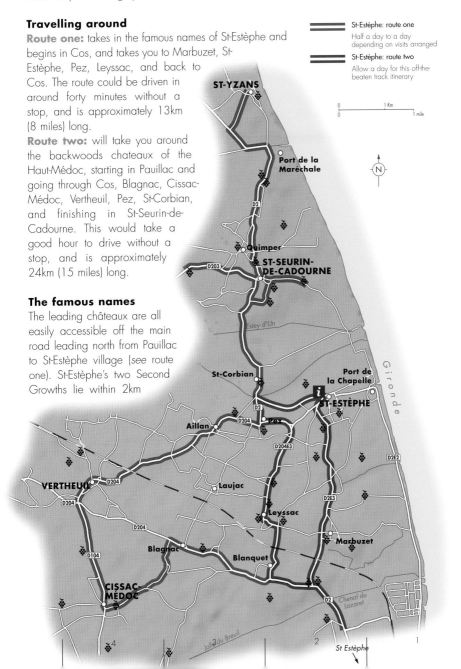

St-Estèphe: route one
Half a day to a day depending on visits arranged

St-Estèphe: route two
Allow a day for this off-the-beaten track itinerary

OTHER THINGS TO DO

Atelier d'Art Yan de Siber
33180 St-Seurin-de-
Cadourne
Tel: 05 56 59 38 55
This gallery offers lots, and
watercolours by local artists.

Château Verdus
33180 St-Seurin-de-
Cadourne
Tel: 05 56 73 13 31
contact@château-verdus.com
www.château-verdus.com
The Dailledouze family's
museum covers the history
of their 500 year tenure.
Entrance fee, under-sixteens
free. Group reductions.
Located east of the D2.

RIGHT *Heading to the beach
from Pauillac and St-Julien is
easy (see directions p.62).*

BELOW *These fishing huts are
used to catch baby prawns
(crevettes), lamprey (lamproie),
shad (alose), and mullet (mulet).*

(1 mile) of each other. First, on high mounds of gravel, is Cos d'Estournel (tel: 05 56 73 15 50, estournel@estournel.com). Its cellar door once opened onto the Sultan of Zanzibar's harem, and behind this diverting oriental-style facade there is a small wine museum here.

Continuing to St-Estèphe along the D2E3, over the railway line and past the hamlet of Marbuzet, is St-Estèphe's other Second Growth, Château Montrose (tel: 05 56 59 30 12), off a side road to the right. Behind its château lie workers' cottages laid out like a mini-village complete with street-names that recall the Alsacien origins of a nineteenth-century proprietor. Montrose (pronounced "mon-rose"; the "t" is silent) is said to have been named after the colour of heather growing on the estate's low hills when in bloom; "mont rose" means "pink hill".

Around Pez

The next right-hand turn leads to the historic Château Meyney, which offers softer, simpler, earlier-maturing wines than Montrose. Just south of St-Estèphe village is Château Phélan-Ségur (see p.53). Its flavourful, but not overpowering, wines are crafted by Champagne Pommery's former owner. The vineyards cover all of St-Estèphe's soil types: sand for lightness, clay for power, limestone for elegance, and gravel for richness. The more imposing seventeenth-century Château Calon-Ségur can be found just to the north. The latter is the most northerly château to have been classified in 1855. Leaving St-Estèphe on the D2E2, turn left at the first crossroads onto the D2 towards the

hamlet of Pez for Château de Pez (*C2*; tel: 05 56 59 30 26), now owned by the excellent Champagne house Roederer. From Pez, head towards the hamlet of Leyssac, past the ugly wine cooperative called La Marquise, and onto Château Pomys with its fine hotel. It is owned by the Arnaud family whose wine interests in St-Estèphe also include Château St-Estephe. Both châteaux produce above average and relatively gentle wines. The three-star hotel is quiet and roomy, but has no restaurant. For more information contact Hotel Pomys (route de Pomeys, Leyssac, 33180 St-Estèphe, tel: 05 56 59 73 44, chateaupomys@aol.com, www.chateaupomys@com). From Château Pomys you can rejoin the D2 if you want to head south to Bordeaux via Pauillac.

The backwoods châteaux
To explore the vineyards bordering St-Estèphe but in the Haut-Médoc appellation, start on the D2 coming from Pauillac, passing the improving St-Estèphe châteaux of Cos-Labory and Lafon-Rochet and passing the historically reliable Château Lilian-Ladouys in the direction of Vertheuil along the D204. After around 3km (1.5 miles) turn left at the hamlet of Blagnac towards Cissac-Médoc, home to some of the Médoc's oldest vineyards, like Château du Breuil. This is owned by Château Cissac (tel: 05 56 59 58 13) which is located next to Cissac's church in the town centre, though you'll find better-value wine if you keep heading west on the route de Gunes to Château d'Osmond (*see right*).

Wine-grower Philippe Tressol studied tropical agriculture before working in Central America and Africa. Now he produces fine-grained, moreish clarets in this small winery. Tressol has been hired by the Bordeaux authorities to teach local wine-growers better vine pruning techniques. Château d'Osmond is signposted from near Cissac's main square.

Woodland trail
From Cissac, head north through the woods along the D104 to Vertheuil with its eleventh-century abbey. Ask at the mayor's office (tel: 05 56 73 30 10) for details of summer exhibitions by local artists and craftsmen held in the old monastery. Next door is Vertheuil's eleventh-century church, said to be one of the finest surviving examples of Romanesque architecture in the Médoc. Both church and abbey had to be partially rebuilt, the church in the fifteenth century and the abbey in the eighteenth century. For details on Vertheuil's barrel-maker *see* p.33.

Some say that First Growth Château Lafite in Pauillac (to the south) took part of its name from the abbot here in 1234, Gombard de Lafite, when the monastic *seigneurie* may well

CHATEAUX IN ST-ESTEPHE

Château d'Aurilhac
Sénilhac
33180 St-Seurin-de-Cadourne
Tel: 05 56 59 35 32 *(D3)*
erik-nieuwaal@wanadoo.fr

Château Grandis
33180 St-Seurin-de-Cadourne
Tel: 05 56 59 31 16 *(D2)*

Château d'Osmond
33250 Cissac
Tel: 05 56 59 59 17 *(A4)*
châteaudosmond@wanadoo.fr

Château Phélan-Ségur
33180 St-Estèphe
Tel: 05 56 59 74 00 *(C2)*
phelan.segur@wanadoo.fr

Château Sociando-Mallet
33180 St-Seurin-de-Cadourne
Tel: 05 56 73 38 80 *(D2)*
scea-jean-gautreau@wanadoo.fr

PRICES: moderate to expensive

WHERE TO STAY

Château Guges
29 rue de la
Croix de Gunes
33250 Cissac
Tel: 05 56 59 58 04
A small property offering
bed and breakfast. It's
closed from December
to February.

Château Papounan
1 rue des Ecoles
Le Bourg
33180 St-Estèphe
Tel: 05 56 59 72 94
Bed and breakfast. There
are four rooms and two
apartments, and it's
located opposite the
pharmacy in St-Estèphe.
English spoken.

Hotel du Midi
Trois Square du Maquis
des Vignes Oudides
33180 St-Seurin-de-
Cadourne
Tel: 05 56 59 30 49
A functional hotel and
good restaurant whose
specialities include
lampreys (*lamproies à
la Bordelaise*) and
Pauillac lamb (*l'agneau
de Pauillac*).

Château Haut Gouat
33180 Vertheuil
Tel: 05 56 41 97 98
An organic vineyard
offering both early drinking
red wines and bed and
breakfast. Located 1.5 km
(1 mile) north of Vertheuil
towards the hamlet of
Bourdin, but south of the
railway line.

Café de l'Abbaye
33180 Vertheuil
Tel: 05 56 41 94 50
This pleasant, small hotel
has four ensuite rooms,
and a bar but no
restaurant.

have included the estate of what is now Château Lafite-Rothschild. From Vertheuil, head to the St-Estèphe hamlet of Pez along the D204 for 3.5km (2 miles) where you rejoin the D2 and the main road to St-Seurin-de-Cadourne.

If you fancy a break, ask at St-Seurin-de-Cadourne's *mairie* (tel: 05 56 59 31 10) for details of the trail set up here in 1997 for ramblers.

The vineyards of the St-Estèphe hamlet of St-Corbian generally disappoint, but St-Seurin-de-Cadourne provides much livelier wines. The finest vineyards here, like Château Grandis and Château Sociando-Mallet (see p.53), are organically inclined, and allow wild grass to grow between the vine rows. This promotes biodiversity, better soil structure, and more complex wines.

Château Sociando-Mallet overlooks the Gironde as it widens to meet the Atlantic just east of St-Seurin, and produces vital, Cabernet Sauvignon-dominated reds. The heart of the Sociando-Mallet vineyards (mainly replanted since 1969) lies on the same type of high, sloping gravel banks over a subsoil of clayey limestone as the famous Château Latour to the south in Pauillac, which also directly faces the Gironde, although Latour's richer gravel makes its wine more powerful – and much more expensive. They are both predominantly Cabernet Sauvignon but Sociando-Mallet's berry fruit softens considerably earlier, after a decade rather than after a generation.

Château Grandis is a rambling estate just north of St-Seurin, east of the D2. The Vergez family have been here since 1857. High-density vines produce generous wines. At Chateau d'Aurilhac (see right) Dutchman Erik Nieuwaal produces firm, well-flavoured reds from an expanding winery 2km (1 mile) from St-Seurin, on the left of the D203.

The Médoc appellation begins 3.5km (2 miles) north on the D2 in the commune of St-Yzans (see Lesparre-Médoc and the Northern Médoc, p.40).

Buying wine in St-Estèphe
In St-Estèphe, the Maison du Vin sells wines by the bottle at the same price as at the châteaux. It provides maps and can arrange visits. Art shows are also held here, mainly in summer. It is open Monday to Friday, 10am–12.30pm and 1.30–5pm and is in the square opposite St-Estèphe's nineteenth-century church with its curious, bottle-shaped spire. (Maison du Vin de St-Estèphe, place de l'Eglise, 33180 St-Estèphe, tel: 05 56 59 30 59, maison-vin.st-estephe@wanadoo.fr)

St-Estèphe wine facts

St-Estèphe is the Médoc's biggest wine commune, with 1,250ha of vines, which is eight per cent of the Médoc vineyard. An average of seven to nine million bottles of St-Estèphe are produced each year.

Only red wines are made, typically blended from Merlot (forty to seventy per cent), Cabernet Sauvignon (thirty to sixty per cent), Cabernet Franc (five to twenty per cent), plus minor amounts of Petit Verdot and Malbec.

There are around seventy-five producers making their own wine, with a further eighty taking their grapes to the cooperative, La Marquise, which is located between the hamlet of Leyssac and St-Estèphe itself.

LEFT *Commercial forestry plots like this can help vineyards by acting as windbreaks against Atlantic squalls.*

WHERE TO EAT

Le Peyrat Restaurant
19 avenue du Littoral
33180 St-Estèphe
Tel: 05 56 59 71 43
This well-run restaurant offers both simple dishes and more gastronomic creations, many prepared from locally grown ingredients. There's a terrace with a view of the Gironde. Closed from August 15 to August 30.

Restaurant de Vertheuil
33180 Vertheuil
Tel: 05 56 41 88 83
Vertheuil's only restaurant offers pretty straightforward fare.

Hotel Café Larrieu
place Mérigot
33180 St-Estèphe
Tel: 05 56 59 30 45
This noisy bar in the centre of St-Estèphe offers quick-service bar food. Although described as an hotel its rudimentary (showerless) rooms are used mainly by labourers.

Pauillac

A s well as being a strategic port and the unofficial capital of the Médoc, Pauillac is considered by aficionados of Bordeaux – and indeed of wine generally – to be the Holy of Holies. It contains three of Planet Wine's most famous châteaux: Latour, Lafite-Rothschild, and Mouton-Rothschild, the last two belonging to separate branches of the famous banking family.

Essence of claret

Pauillac's Cabernet Sauvignon-dominated red wines are said to be the epitome of claret: deep but not opaque in colo ur, and with powerful flavours of ripe backcurrants which turn to cedar, clove, mint, cigar box, and lead pencil with a decade or more of age. The vines thrive on deep mounds of sandy gravel which rise either side of the town, which is a sprawling mix of quiet back streets and lorry-laden main roads, with a pretty port and an ugly (but disused) oil refinery.

Most château-owners are absentee landlords, resident in Paris or the city of Bordeaux, so the best chance of meeting the locals who work the vines and clean the barrels is at the covered market every Saturday in place Gabriel Gachet.

BELOW *The Renaissance-style Château Pichon-Longueville-Baron is one of the Médoc's most iconic.*

4   3   2   1

Map labels:

↑ St Estèphe

Chenal du Lazaret

D2

Jalle du Breuil

Milon

Mousset

D2

Loubeyres

Le Pouyalet

les Carruades

D205

Padarnac

Lescargean

D205

Guérin

Labrousse

Pibran

D205

St-Sauveur

Gironde

Ste-Croix

PAUILLAC

le Fournas

D104

la Naude

Artigues

D104

Bages

D206

les Gabarreys

D2

St-Lambert

Daubos

St-Julien

D2

N

A
B
C
D
E

Local rivalry

Pauillac's renown has bred simmering rivalries in its wine elite ever since vineyards came to dominate here in the late seventeenth century. The Rothschild estates of Mouton and Lafite vie with each other, and with Latour.

In the south, meanwhile, the two Pichon estates face each other across the main D2 road: the Baron with its modern, oaky, fruit-driven winemaking style versus the more demure, classic Comtesse.

Getting there

By car from the centre of Bordeaux it is 54km (34 miles) to Pauillac on the D2. The journey takes less than one hour. Try to avoid the weekend of the Bordeaux marathon which takes place each September and begins on the quayside in Pauillac.

By train, go from Gare St-Jean in Bordeaux to the station in Pauillac (2 place de Verdun). The railway station is on the north side of the town. By bus, take CITRAM Aquitaine buses from place des Quinconces in the centre of Bordeaux (Ligne 705).

Travelling around

Just 24km (15 miles) in length, this route would take just thirty to sixty minutes with no stops. But, to make the most of visiting here allow the best part of a day. This itinerary goes from the two Pichon estates south of Daubos, to Bages hamlet, Pauillac's quayside, Le Pouyalet plateau, Carruades plateau, St-Sauveur, the hamlets of Le Fournas and Artigues, then on to Daubos.

━━━ Pauillac
Take the best part of a day for this route

0 ———— 1 Km
0 ———— 1 mile

Towering achievement

The first châteaux one encounters when approaching Pauillac from St-Julien and the south up the D2 are the two Pichons and Château Latour (www.château-latour.com). The original tower from which Latour takes its name was razed in the middle ages. The tower in the vineyards today is a dovecote, built in 1860.

Of the two Pichons, only Château Pichon-Baron(on the left-hand side of the D2) has permanent staff on hand for visitors (see p.60). There are free daily guided tours of this turreted, showpiece château, which was built in 1851, and its sparkling, marble-floored winery, built rather more recently. There is free tasting, but a small fee is payable for groups of fifteen or more. Meanwhile opposite at Pichon Comtesse (www.pichon.lalande.com) a prior appointment is necessary.

Lunch bags

Continue towards Pauillac and the hamlet of Bages for Château Lynch-Bages, or "lunch bags" as the Americans have nicknamed it (D1; tel: 05 56 73 24 00, infochato@lynchbages.com). It was said to have had a berry-scented aroma in the past – from a cellarmaster who rinsed the barrels with blackcurrant liqueur.

Also in Bages is the luxury Cordeillan-Bages hotel (see p.61). From Bages head towards the Gironde, and then follow the shore road north along the quays for a selection of hotels and the tourist office (see right).

A largely unlovely town

A disused oil refinery to the north, congested roads with often tight turns to negotiate, the constant rumble of lorries laden with pallets of wine, and some scrappy architecture in its centre hardly make the town of Pauillac a thing of beauty.

Yet, Pauillac is a major population centre, in Médoc terms at least, with 6,000-odd inhabitants – more than St-Julien, St-Estèphe, and Margaux combined. This makes Pauillac a useful place to stop: there are four pharmacies, over half a dozen banks with hole-in-the-wall facilities, a post office, and a good range of shops selling everything from flowers to fashion accessories.

Blending in

Pauillac's size helps make visitors feel a bit more anonymous here than in St-Julien to the south or St-Emilion across the Gironde. And local events not specifically geared to wine make Pauillac seem just like any other French town. For example, you can buy locally produced goods like pottery, paintings, and metalwork at the evening markets held at the Port de Plaisance in August (details from the Maison du Vin).

Don't miss this

Whatever you think of its wine, Château Mouton-Rothschild's amazing wine museum is one of Bordeaux's absolute must-see wine attractions (see p.60).

Mouton's former owner, Baron Philippe de Rothschild (1902–88), opened his private museum here in 1962. Artefacts are drawn from the last 3,000 years and show how wine and art relate. There are works by some of the modern artists chosen to design the Mouton labels (their payment is 120 bottles). This tradition began in 1924 when Mouton became the first leading Médoc estate to bottle its own wine rather than leaving the job to sometimes unscrupulous merchants. Delft pottery, Ming vases, Venetian glasswork, tapestries, pre-Columbian sculptures, and Persian drinking vessels from the eighth and ninth centuries BC are beautifully presented. The museum is open by appointment only and closed during August, weekends, and public holidays.

ABOVE The Château at Pichon-Lalande dates from the 1840s, and overlooks Château Latour.

LEFT A number of golf courses are hidden among the Landes pine forests (see p.80 for details).

The Pouyalet plateau

Rejoin the D2 road north of the town near the railway station to head up onto the Pouyalet plateau. The gravel under the vines here is up to 30m (98 feet) deep – a paradise for the late-ripening Cabernet Sauvignon, which benefits from the heat reflected by the stones.

Spot Lafite

If you stay on the D2 you will see Château Lafite-Rothschild (www.lafite.com), the last Pauillac château before St-Estèphe. The view, across low-lying parkland, of the château's sixteenth-century turret is partially obscured by the trees.

You will have to book in advance for a chance to see the circular, underground barrel-cellar here (the house is closed to visitors) and the wine library or vinotheque, containing bottles of Lafite back to 1787.

As Lafite comes into view take the right-hand turn off the D2, direction Mousset, to reach Château La Fleur-Milon (see p.60). This is one of Pauillac's better minor estates, boasting small plots of vines intermingled with those of more famous châteaux.

Behind the Gironde estuary

To access those Pauillac vineyards that are set back from the Gironde estuary, towards the Haut-Médoc commune of St-

RIGHT *The two Pichon estates – this is Pichon-Baron – were dividied in 1850; until then they formed one property.*

CHATEAUX IN PAUILLAC

Château La Fleur-Milon
Le Pouyalet
33250 Pauillac
Tel: 05 56 59 29 01 *(B1)*
contact@lafleurmilon.com

Château Pichon-Longueville-Baron
33250 Pauillac
Tel: 05 56 73 17 17 *(E1)*
infochato@pichonlongueville
.com

Château Pontet-Canet
33250 Pauillac
Tel: 05 56 59 04 04 *(C2)*
pontet-canet@wanadoo.fr

Château Mouton-Rothschild
33250 Pauillac
Tel: 05 56 59 22 22 *(B2)*
webmaster@bpdr.com

PRICES: expensive

Sauveur, take the left-hand fork in the D2 on the D205, just north of the Pauillac railway station. This road takes you across the Carruades plateau whose vines are the backbone of Lafite.

The first estate signposted on the left of the D205 is Château Pontet-Canet which dates from the early eighteenth century (*see left*). Tours take in its beautiful first-floor fermentation rooms, complete with batteries of wooden vats (although these are no longer used), from where the new wine could be run via gravity into barrel. The wine is one of the most improved in Bordeaux in recent years. The owners, the Tesserons, have also upped quality at their other vineyard across the Jalle du Breuil in St-Estèphe, Lafon-Rochet.

Twin towers of Peyrabon

From Pontet-Canet, staying on the D205 eventually takes you to Cissac (*see* St-Estèphe). If you bear left at the five-way crossroads (E2) just over 3km (two miles) from the railway station, direction Guérin, you pick up signs to two of St-Sauveur's more consistent estates: Château Liversan (C4), tel: 05 56 59 57 07) and Château Peyrabon ((C4), tel: 05 56 59 57 10), with its distinctive twin towers. Peyrabon boasts a music room in which Queen Victoria once attended a concert.

From Liversan and Peyrabon, pick up the D104 towards the hamlets of Le Fournas and Artigues. In Le Fournas, Château Hourtin-Ducasse (tel: 05 56 59 56 92) offers rather firm reds but at generally fair prices. Still on the D104, after Artigues, Château Grand-Puy-Lacoste (*D2*, tel: 05 56 59 06 66)

appears on the left-hand side. It is owned by the Borie family, proprietors of Château Ducru-Beaucaillou in St-Julien. The château was built in 1850, against the original house, which dates from 1737. "Grand Puy" means "big mound" and refers to the gravel ridges either side of Artigues. Wines from another Grand Puy estate, Grand-Puy-Ducasse (tel: 05 56 11 29 00) are made in cellars near the port, on the quays.

From Artigues, head towards the Gironde and turn right onto the D206 to reach Château Batailley (*D2*, tel: 05 55 00 00 70). The park here was designed by Napoleon III's landscape gardener, Barillet-Deschamp, and contains mature trees from all over the world.

Batailley's name is thought to come from a battle fought against the English during the Hundred Years' War. Batailley once formed part of a larger domaine, but was divided in 1942, when what is now Château Haut-Batailley (tel: 05 56 73 16 73) was hived off. The vineyard contains a tower, La Tour d'Aspic, after which Haut-Batailley's above-average second wine is named. From Haut-Batailley one can rejoin the D2 to head back to Bordeaux by traversing the hamlet of Daubos, slightly to the north of the Pichons and Château Latour.

Wine shops

Pauillac's renown means that none of the top châteaux need sell direct to the public, but you can pick up wines from local wine shops like Caves des Mets d'Oc (68 rue du Maréchale Joffre, tel: 05 56 59 15 91, www.metsdoc.com), on the main D2 Bordeaux-Pauillac road. Or try the bigger Pavillon des Châteaux (5 quai Albert Pichon, tel: 05 56 59 17 84), which is open 10am–7pm, April to September, and has a good selection of wine paraphernalia, like carafes and corkscrews, as well as older vintages from Pauillac private cellars that have never left the village.

Take to the water

Boat trips on the Gironde estuary are organized by Pauillac's Maison du Tourisme et du Vin (*see* p.59). The barges or sailing boats leave from Pauillac's harbour. The barge trip sometimes lands on Patiras island, whose vineyards are part of the commune of Pauillac, but whose (not very good) wine can be sold only under the generic Bordeaux appellation. The nearest Atlantic

beach to this part of the Médoc is Hourtin-Plage. Take the D4 from the N215 Bordeaux-Lesparre road to Hourtin-Plage via the town of Hourtin, a journey of 30km (19 miles).

Walking routes

Pauillac's Maison du Tourisme has organised a 21km (13-mile) ramblers' route (follow yellow markers) which passes châteaux in the north of Pauillac like Pibran, Pontet-Canet, and Mouton-Rothschild, but very few in the southern part of the commune. The route begins outside the Maison du Tourisme's office on Pauillac's quayside.

Back to school

Château Lynch-Bages (D1; tel: 05 56 73 19 33) runs a wine school for both professionals and members of the public (French, English or German are spoken). The ninety-minute courses can be tailormade, even at fairly short notice, for groups or individuals but usually consist of "The basics of wine-tasting", on the vocabulary of wine appreciation (four vintages of Lynch-Bages are tasted); "Grape varieties", on Cabernet Sauvignon, Merlot, Cabernet Franc, and Petit Verdot, with students making their own blend at the end; and "Les grands crus" in which four *grands crus* from different Bordeaux regions such as St-Emilion, Pomerol and the Médoc are tasted. Ecole du Bordeaux wine courses and cooking courses are also held in the city of Bordeaux at 7 rue du Château Trompette (off place Tourny; tel: 05 56 90 91 92, contact@ecoledubordeaux.com).

Local lambs

Pauillac's gastronomic speciality is *agneau de Pauillac*, now defined as baby lamb fed only on ewe's milk, but not necessarily in Pauillac. Locally produced meat comes from animals grazed on the salt marshes by the Gironde. Their almost white meat is soft and delicately flavoured. To see how the animals are raised, make an appointment to visit the Reyes family's Bergerie des Grands Crus (tel: 05 56 59 22 72), in St-Lambert in the south of Pauillac near Château Latour.

Seasonal highlights

Pauillac hosts a number of festivals each year, including a carnival in March. Portes Ouvertes (Open Doors) is held at the châteaux in April. May sees the Pentecost regatta, which can be viewed from the Pauillac quayside, and the festival of Pauillac lamb (see above). There is a music festival in June bringing together reggae, rock, jazz, and classical, and a festival of wine and terroir in July. Throughout July and August films are screened at an open-air cinema. More energetically, the Bordeaux Marathon takes place in September, starting on

WHERE TO EAT

Le Mascaret
2 quai Léon Perrier
33250 Pauillac
Tel: 05 57 75 29 18
Formal seafood restaurant on the quays featuring shad (*alose*), lamprey (*lamproie*), mullet (*mulet*), plaice (*carrelet*), perch (*perche*) and the highly sought after baby eels (*pibales*).

Le Pauillac
2 quai Albert Pichon
33250 Pauillac
Tel: 05 56 59 19 20
Bordeaux staples here include Pauillac lamb, duck breast (*magret de canard*) and duck confit (*confit de canard*).

Le Cabernet
7 rue Aristide Briand
33250 Pauillac
Tel: 05 56 59 26 04
Value-for-money *créperie* – a good place to stop for those passing through.

L'Aperception
5 quai Léon Perrier
33250 Pauillac
Tel: 05 56 59 19 82
Serious, filling rib steak grilled on vine prunings.

the quayside in Pauillac. A new tradition began in 2004 with "*repas de vendanges*" or harvest meals; in this case a sit-down beef stew (*pot au feu*) lunch offered by Château Lynch-Bages.

Pauillac wine facts

Pauillac produces between six and seven million bottles of red wine each year, from around 1,200ha of vines. There are around forty wineries, most producing a second and often a third wine as well as the château wine. Another seventy-five smaller growers take their grapes to the Cave Coopérative la Rose Pauillac. A typical wine is blended from Cabernet Sauvignon (around sixty-five to eighty per cent or more) plus Cabernet Franc (up to twenty-five per cent), and Merlot and Petit Verdot (up to twenty per cent combined).

The 1855 Classification gave Pauillac the largest number of Classed Growths (eighteen) of any appellation, and the most fifths (twelve), but no third growths. This division merely reflected the market values of Pauillac wines as traded by the brokers in 1855 and in the years before the classification was drawn up. Since then, the classified estates have steadily bought up smaller vineyards, so today over eighty per cent of the vineyard belongs to châteaux classified in 1855: Latour, Lafite-Rothschild (First Growths); Mouton-Rothschild, Pichon-Longueville Comtesse de Lalande, Pichon-Longueville-Baron (Second Growths); Duhart-Milon-Rothschild (Fourth Growth); d'Armailhac, Batailley, Clerc-Milon, Croizet-Bages, Grand-Puy-Ducasse, Grand-Puy-Lacoste, Haut-Bages-Libéral, Haut-Batailley, Lynch-Bages, Lynch-Moussas, Pédesclaux, Pontet-Canet (Fifth Growths). Château Mouton-Rothschild was upgraded to First Growth in 1973.

CAMPING

Camping Les Gabarreys
route de la Rivière
33250 Pauillac
Tel: 05 56 59 10 03
camping.les.
gabarreys@wanadoo.fr
Pauillac's campsite is open March-October. Head north from St-Julien on the D2, and after the tower of Château Latour appears on your right, take the first right onto the RD2/E6/ route de la Rivière, and the campsite is situated between the road and the Gironde estuary.

LEFT *Lampreys in a bucket: beware of a surfeit.*

BELOW *The Landes forests between the vineyards and the Atlantic help prevent the dramatic temperature fluctuations that vines find so stressful.*

St-Julien

Approach St-Julien from the south via Cussac across fertile pastures interspersed with woodland, and you have no idea that you are entering one of Bordeaux's most revered wine regions. St-Julien is so highly regarded that the huge, tacky wine bottle painted with the village name that greets those travelling up the D2 from Bordeaux could be seen as a modest, if clumsy, attempt to disguise its greatness.

RIGHT *Vineyards give way to arable crops the closer one gets to the Gironde estuary.*

BELOW *Nudity is fine for statues and nudist beaches; dress code for châteaux visits is smart casual.*

Plan ahead

Be warned, though. Apart from wine there is little here of interest for tourists. Visitors wanting to sample the greatest wines must make prior appointments to be guaranteed a welcome and a wine sample. Casual visitors should stick to St-Julien's more mundane wineries, or head inland to the slightly less noble Haut-Médoc vineyards in the village of St-Laurent.

Small and beautifully formed

Whereas Margaux covers five communes, St-Estèphe half a dozen hamlets and Pauillac splits between two extremes either side of the town, St-Julien is both small and relatively homogeneous. However, there are three quite distinct parts.

In the south lies the Beychevelle plateau upon which stretch the classed-growth vineyards of Châteaux Beychevelle, Branaire with its eighteenth-century *orangerie*, and Ducru-Beaucaillou, with Gruaud-Larose overlooking them from the southwest. Clay-gravel topsoils over limestone gives wines whose tight core gains broad, boxing-glove softness with age.

In the north across a small valley is the Léoville plateau, a rich rib of sandy gravels over iron-rich sandstone, resembling southern Pauillac immediately to the north (*see p.57*). The taste, smell and colour of Léoville's three main vineyards, Léoville-Barton, Léoville-Las-Cases, and Léoville-Poyferré are very similar to southern Pauillacs like Latour and the Pichons just to the north: blackcurrant-scented wines that taste of cedar.

The separate fingers of the St-Julien and Beychevelle plateaux extend inland, to the knuckle of a third plateau, at St-Laurent. Here, the wines lack the elegance of the best St-Juliens because the soils are more clayey, but they also have less exalted price tags.

The St-Julien appellation incorporates two hamlets: the sixteenth-century Beychevelle and the much older, seventh-century St-Julien, sometimes confusingly called St-Julien-de-Beychevelle. St-Julien was the first wine region in Bordeaux to process waste-water from its larger wineries in an

environmentally friendly fashion – it is said to take the equivalent of seven bottles of water to make one bottle of wine.

St-Julian wine facts

St-Julien produces between five and seven million bottles of red wine each year from around 900ha of vines. Over eighty-five per cent of the vineyard land here belongs to classed-growth châteaux; in fact, St-Julien has the most classed growths (eleven) of any appellation bar Pauillac, but no First or Fifth Growths. In 1855, the following estates were classified: Châteaux Léoville-Las-Cases, Léoville-Poyferré, Léoville-Barton, Gruaud-Larose, and Ducru-Beaucaillou (Second Growths); Lagrange and Langoa-Barton (Third Growths); St-Pierre, Branaire, Talbot, and Beychevelle (Fourth Growths).

Today, there are around forty wineries, most producing a second and even a third wine as well as the château wine. A typical wine is blended from Cabernet Sauvignon (around sixty to seventy per cent) plus Merlot (up to forty per cent), Cabernet Franc and Petit Verdot (up to fifteen per cent combined).

Getting there

By car from the Bordeaux ring road it is 45km (28 miles) to St-Julien. The journey takes less than an hour on the D2 or via St-Laurent on the N215. Alternatively, take CITRAM Aquitaine buses from Place des Quinconces in Bordeaux centre, destination Pauillac (Ligne 705). The St-Laurent railway station is no longer in use. Take trains to Pauillac instead.

CAMPING

Camping Le Paradis
8 rue A Fourthon
33112 St-Laurent-et-Benon
Tel: 05 56 59 42 15
Mobile: 06 87 73 66 36
Located on the N215 Bordeaux-Lesparre road, just north of St-Laurent. There's a swimming pool, plus caravan and camping, and bicycle hire.

CHATEAUX IN ST-JULIEN

. . . .

Château Beychevelle
33250 St-Julien-de-
Beychevelle
Tel: 05 56 73 20 70 *(C1)*
beychevelle@beychevelle.com
www.beychevelle.com

Château de la Bridane
33250 St-Julien
Tel: 05 56 59 91 70 *(D2)*
www.vignobles-saintout.com

Domaine de Cartujac
33112 St-Laurent-et-Benon
Tel: 05 56 59 91 70 *(B6)*
www.vignobles-saintout.com

Château Lagrange
33250 St-Julien-de-
Beychevelle
Tel: 05 56 73 38 38 *(C3)*
chateau-lagrange@château-
lagrange.com
www.chateau-lagrange.com

Château Larose-Trintaudon
route de Pauillac (D206)
33112 St-Laurent-et-Benon
Tel: 05 56 59 41 72 *(D3)*
info@trintaudon.com

Château Léoville-Barton
33250 St-Julien
Tel: 05 56 59 06 05 *(D3)*
chateau@leoville-barton.com

PRICES: expensive

BELOW *Forestry is a major*
employer in the Médoc
peninsula.

Travelling around

This route is about 24km (15 miles) in length. It starts in Beychevelle and goes to the Léoville plateau, St-Julien-de-Beychevelle, St-Laurent-Médoc, Cartujac and back to Beychevelle. If just driving around, it would take about an hour.

Château Beychevelle

Approaching the hamlet of Beychevelle from the south on the D2 one passes Château Beychevelle on the right (*see* left). Beychevelle is a corruption of the French for "lower sails": *baisse voile* (or *bacha velo* in Gascon). This is what ships on their way to Bordeaux had to do to salute the (then) medieval fort under its sixteenth-century owner, the Admiral of France. Beychevelle's current château was built in the eighteenth century and is best viewed from the Gironde side rather than from the D2. Free visits (without tasting) last one hour. Book ahead to be sure of a place; Beychevelle receives over 25,000 visitors annually. On the left is the unpretentious Château Branaire (www.branaire.com), which in 1666 was hived off from Château Beychevelle after its owner died with large debts. Branaire's current owner heads France's biggest sugar-refining conglomerate.

Along the Gironde

Stay on the D2, and the view on the right is of tightly planted vineyards, a luxuriant strip of low-lying marsh and grazing land, and the Gironde. The landscape also reveals the squat, nineteenth-century towers of Château Ducru-Beaucaillou (tel: 05 56 73 16 73). These now cover a modern, squeaky-clean underground cellar – rare in the Médoc where the water table is generally so high.

"Irish Tom" Barton

As the D2 dips away from the Beychevelle plateau, just after the turning to Ducru-Beaucaillou, Château Langoa-Barton appears almost tucked away on the left. This is the headquarters for nearby Château Léoville-Barton (*see* left), which is under the same ownership. This estate was part of Château Léoville-Las-Cases until after the Revolution when the descendants of wine merchant "Irish Tom" Barton acquired it. It's still owned by the Barton family, and is probably Bordeaux's best-value Second Growth. There's no actual château building for Léoville-Barton, so Château Langoa-Barton is used instead. The single-storey château covers underground cellars, and

Marcillan

Cartujac

D104

Bernos

Benon

there are terraced gardens behind. There are free visits and tastings by prior appointment on weekdays and it is closed on Friday afternoons.

Revolutionary vineyards

The road then rises quickly onto the Léoville plateau and the hamlet of St-Julien. On the right the walled vineyards belong to the Second Growth château, Léoville-Las-Cases (tel: 05 56 73 25 26). This was created after the Revolution when the Marquis de Las-Cases fled the guillotine. His estate was divided in three: Châteaux Léoville-Barton, Léoville-Poyferré and Léoville-Las-Cases.

The Marquis de Las-Cases's descendants added a walled arch with his name to the 50ha vineyard called Le Grand Enclos. Its image features on Las-Cases's

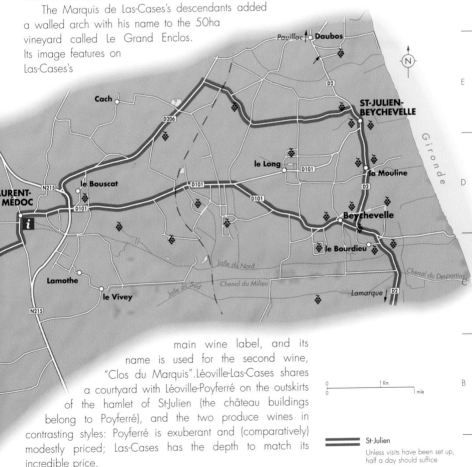

main wine label, and its name is used for the second wine, "Clos du Marquis".Léoville-Las-Cases shares a courtyard with Léoville-Poyferré on the outskirts of the hamlet of St-Julien (the château buildings belong to Poyferré), and the two produce wines in contrasting styles: Poyferré is exuberant and (comparatively) modestly priced; Las-Cases has the depth to match its incredible price.

St-Julien

Unless visits have been set up, half a day should suffice

Around the Léoville plateau

The less exalted but welcoming Château La Bridane lies just north of St-Julien on the D2 towards Pauillac (see left). La

Bridane offers free visits to the winery and barrel cellar, with free tasting – June 28 to September 6 on weekdays, and on Saturdays 10–12am and 2–6pm. It is closed on Sundays. The large parking area means that La Bridane is popular with coach parties. The château is run by the Saintout family who also owns Domaine de Cartujac (see below).

Before La Bridane, take the first left to cross the Léoville plateau, through vineyards belonging mainly to Léoville-Poyferré, and head towards the D206 St-Laurent-Pauillac road. Turn left at the (dangerous) T-junction towards St-Laurent. The first winery on the left is Château Larose-Trintaudon (see p.66). This is the largest vineyard in the Haut-Médoc appellation. Vines here ripen up to one week later than those closer to the Gironde estuary, and the wines are less smooth as a result. The château offers free tastings and visits, by prior appointment.

A drive through St-Laurent on the D104 towards Carcans and the Atlantic brings you to Domaine de Cartujac (see p.66). After less than 1.6km (1 mile), turn right, making sure you follow signs to Cartujac, otherwise the road becomes a dead-end in the Landes forests. The Saintout family produces chunky, Merlot-dominated reds from its two cellars, Château de la Bridane in St-Julien (see above) and Domaine de Cartujac. The domaine is open Monday to Friday 9–12am, and 2–6pm, except Wednesday mornings.

RIGHT *St-Julien's gravel peters out at the Gironde estuary's shoreline.*

BELOW *The stone arch marking Château Leoville-Las-Cases' best plot, "Le Grand Clos".*

Battles and knights

Head back to Beychevelle along the D101 St-Laurent-Beychevelle road. On the left is the moated, thirteenth-century Château la Tour-Carnet (D4, tel: 05 56 59 40 13), an improving Fourth Growth and the oldest estate in St-Laurent-Médoc. The hamlet of Benon to the southwest sometimes has its name appended to St-Laurent-Médoc, and centres on its twelfth-century church, Notre Dame de Benon. This was a former staging post for the Maltese Knights.

The next three right-hand turns reveal three huge vineyards of roughly 100ha each: Château de Camensac (tel: 05 56 59 41 69), Château Belgrave (tel: 05 56 35 53 00), and Château Lagrange (see p.66). Lagrange – St-Julien's largest vineyard (113ha) belonged to the Knights Templar in the middle ages, but now produces refreshing Cabernet Sauvignon-dominated reds under the Japanese Suntory group, owners here since 1983. Free visits

WHERE TO STAY AND EAT

Hotel Restaurant la Renaissance
rue du Général de Gaulle
33112 St-Laurent-et-Benon
Tel: 05 56 59 40 29
Now that Le Lion d'Or has closed, this is the only local hotel. There are eight rooms, of which two are ensuite. There's traditional family cooking in the restaurant.

Restaurant le St-Julien
11 rue de St-Julien
33250 St-Julien
Tel: 05 56 59 63 87
Claude Broussard's restaurant is located in the hamlet of St-Julien, in a former bakery dating from 1850. Atmospheric bare stone walls and open beams complement seasonal dishes like lamprey, Pauillac lamb, asparagus and shad (*alose*). Don't confuse with pricier:

Le Relais de St-Julien
30 rue de St-Julien
Tel: 05 56 59 63 87

La Pizzeria Chez Fredo
rue du Général de Gaulle
33112 St-Laurent-et-Benon
Tel: 05 56 59 46 96
A useful place for a quick snack roughly two-thirds of the way between Bordeaux and Lesparre.

Restaurant la Veranda
18 rue Pierre Castera
33112 St-Laurent-et-Benon
Tel: 05 56 59 96 96
There's a three-course set menu for lunch. It's open in the evening only by prior reservation and for groups.

by appointment on weekdays include a tasting of Château Lagrange and of its second wine, Les Fiefs. Initially, the French government was reluctant to see one of Bordeaux's leading vineyards fall into foreign hands, and stipulated the sale could only go ahead if Suntory was prepared to invest massively in awaking this sleeping giant. Suntory replanted those vineyards containing too much Merlot, and built a new air-conditioned winery and barrel hall.

Finishing off

A little further on the right is Château Gruaud-Larose (*C2*; tel: 05 56 73 15 20, contact@château-gruaud-larose.com). It produces a solidly performing wine but has recently been showing more flair, and is proving its worth as the best-sited vineyard on the Beychevelle plateau.

Fourth Growth Château Talbot (www.château-talbot.com) lies down the last major turn on the left before the hamlet of Beychevelle is reached. The estate is named after the English earl John Talbot, who died in 1453 at the battle of Castillon, the battle which ended the Hundred Years' War. Gruaud-Larose and Talbot were both owned by the merchant Cordier from 1934–1993. Gruaud Larose was sold to the rival vineyard-owning group Taillan, and Talbot remained with the descendants of the Cordier family.

In the hamlet of Beychevelle are Château St-Pierre (under the same ownership as Château Gloria) and the infuriatingly inconsistent *cru bourgeois* Château Terrey-Gros-Cailloux (not open to the public). From here the D101 joins the D2 back to Bordeaux.

Cooling down

If you are in the mood for a swim, the nearest beach from this part of the Médoc is Carcans-Plage. It can be reached by taking the D104 off the N215 Bordeaux-Lesparre road at St-Laurent-Médoc. The journey is around 35km (22 miles), via the town of Carcans.

Listrac, Moulis, and central Médoc

This part of the Médoc is the often-ignored stepping-stone between the more illustrious vineyards of Margaux to the south and St-Julien to the north. Apart from the medieval Château de Lamarque (*see* p.74) most of the châteaux are *maisons bourgeoises*, middle-class country houses dating from the mid-nineteenth century when the region enjoyed its biggest boom. Travellers hurrying through here on the Gironde-hugging D2 or on the forested N215/D1 further inland should consider stopping here, for this is the single largest area in the Haut-Médoc where serious bargains can be found.

A miller's tale

It seems hard to believe today that this central part of the Médoc peninsula was historically wheat-growing country. Wheat was ground in windmills, two of which remain: the Moulin Puy-Minjon which can be seen on the right-hand side of the D5 heading from Moulis-en-Médoc towards the hamlet of Bouqueyran, and the ruined Moulin de Tiquetorte which dates from the tenth century and which is a short walk south of Moulis-en-Médoc (there is a car park here). The name of Moulis is in fact a corruption of *moulins*, French for "mills".

BELOW *Trees this time, not vines, pruned ready for spring. Everything gets pruned in Bordeaux.*

The pebbled soil proved so infuriating to locals wishing to grow corn here that Château Maucaillou in Moulis (*see* p.74) was given its name from *mauvais cailloux* or "bad pebbles". Later this free-draining soil was seen as perfect for vines.

It has also become a target for gravel quarrying for use mainly in road building: winegrowers in Avensan have had a running courtroom battle with excavators whose noisy diggers usually work behind screens of pine trees in the Landes forests. The quarrying leaves gaping holes in the landscape and ruins prime vineyard land – all hidden from view.

Defensive manouevres

However, battles of a more visceral kind have been fought here. The fortress directly overlooking the Gironde at Vieux

Cussac ("Old Cussac") dates from 1690 and formed part of a defensive battle line across the estuary, with similar forts at Blaye on the opposite bank and on the Isle Paté in the middle of the river.

Central Médoc
Half a day to a day should be enough, depending on what visits are arranged

Getting there
By car from the Bordeaux ring road it is 40km (25 miles) to Lamarque on the D2, or to Listrac via the N215/D1. The journey takes less than forty-five minutes. By ferry, you can access this part of the Haut-Médoc from Blaye on the other side of the Gironde estuary by using the Blaye-Lamarque ferry. The journey takes less than thirty minutes. There are four to five crossings in each direction daily. *See* www.bernezac.com for further details.

Travelling around
This 48km (30-mile) route takes us from Arcins up to Lamarque, Vieux Cussac, Cussac-Fort-Médoc, down to Grand Poujeaux, southwest to Moulis-en-Médoc, back to Medrac, Listrac-Médoc, and Bouqueyran.

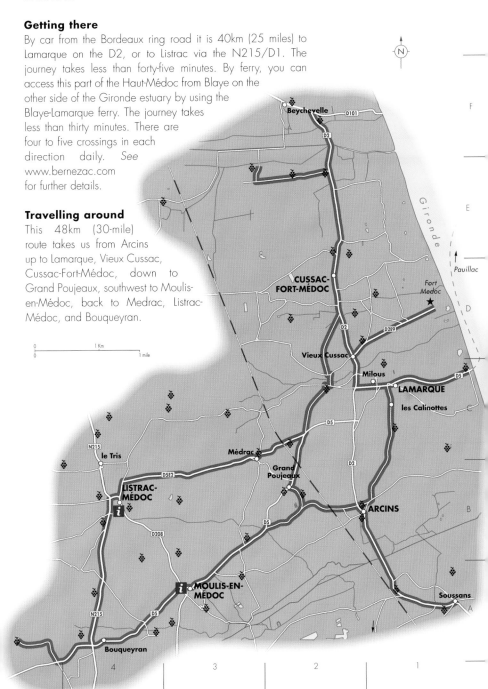

WHERE TO STAY AND EAT
. . . .

Auberge des Vignerons
28 avenue de Soulac
33480 Listrac
Tel: 05 56 58 08 68
This restaurant with
comfortable rooms, in
a former wine cellar next
to the Maison des Vins
in Listrac, has a terrace
overlooking the vines.
Salmon, crayfish, foie gras,
and chocolate tart are
recommended. An excellent
wine list makes this the local
growers' favourite. Closed
February, and for Saturday
lunch, Sunday dinner, and
every Monday from October
to May.

Auberge Médocain
13 place du Maréchal Juin
33480 Listrac
Tel: 05 56 58 08 86
No-frills rooms plus a simple
restaurant located off Listrac's
main square, opposite the
pharmacy. Previously
called the Hôtel de France.
Local snails and eel are
specialities.

Le Lion d'Or
place République
33460 Arcins
Tel: 05 56 58 96 79
Popular and very busy
restaurant between the
Margaux and St-Julien
appellations, and
conveniently located off
the D2. Good value daily
fixed menu. Closed July,
December 24 to January 1,
Sundays, Mondays, and
public holidays.

Le Relais du Médoc
33460 Lamarque
Tel: 05 56 58 92 27
Uncomplicated regional
cooking and a few rooms for
those who missed the last
Lamarque-Blaye ferry.

Around Arcins

The communes of Arcins, Lamarque, and Cussac all overlook
the Gironde estuary, and lie on the D2 which links Soussans in
the Margaux appellation to the south with the hamlet of
Beychevelle in the St-Julien appellation to the north. Some of the
small estates here signpost free tastings ("*accueil*") and direct
sale ("*vente directe*"), and provide easy parking for those
wishing to fill their car boots.

In Arcins, take the right-hand fork, direction Château
Malescasse (tel: 05 56 58 90 09), rather than the D2, as this
route will take you into the centre of Lamarque from where it is
easier to reach Château de Lamarque (*see* p.74). Construction
of this haunting medieval fortress overloking the Gironde from
northeast of Lamarque began in the eleventh and twelfth
centuries under the French, and was completed by the English
during their occupation of Aquitaine in the fourteenth century
before the Hundred Years' War. Both Henry IV and the Duke of
Gloucester stayed here. Visits by appointment.

The short road leading to the Lamarque-Blaye ferry can be
easily reached from here. Immediately north of Lamarque is
Cussac, divided into Vieux Cussac and the more built-up
Cussac-Fort about 300m (980 feet) to the north.

To reach Cussac's ruined fort, turn right in the middle of
Vieux Cussac onto the the D2E9 towards the Gironde.

Further north

Continuing north from Vieux Cussac to Cussac-Fort-Médoc on
the D2 takes one past signs to the pedestrian Château Aney
(tel: 05 56 58 94 89), the improving Château du Raux, and
the well-sited Château Lamothe-Bergeron (tel: 05 56 01 30
10), all on the right-hand or Gironde side. "*Lamothe*" is local
dialect for "the hill", in this case a bed of gravel with woodland,
vines, and Lamothe-Bergeron's recently renovated château.

To reach Château Lanessan (*see* p.74), take the last left-
hand turn before the border with St-Julien, 2.4km (1.5 miles)
north of Cussac-Fort-Medoc. Lanessan's core vineyard occupies
probably the greatest site between Margaux and St Julien (other,
less auspicious sites have been added, though). Paying visitors
receive a winery tour and a tasting, plus a tour of Lanessan's
carriage and harness museum and stables

Visiting Grand Poujeaux

The best place to start exploring vineyards set further back
from the Gironde is in the sub-region of Moulis called Grand
Poujeaux, where many local vineyards have the word
"Poujeaux" appended to their names. One exception is the
highly regarded Château Chasse-Spleen (B2, tel: 05 56 58
02 37, info@chasse-spleen.com for visits by appointment).

At Château Granins-Grand-Poujeaux (*see* p.74), Pascal and Marie-Lyn Bodin make good-value Moulis reds at their small winery in the centre of Grand Poujeaux. Coming from Cussac on the D5 you take the second turning on the right after Château Poujeaux.

Grand Poujeaux hamlet is 1.6km (1 mile) due west of the centre of Arcins. If you are coming from there, head north on the D2 turning left at the second main crossroads in Arcins, and cross the railway line. This road will take you south of Grand Poujeaux and then to Moulis-en-Médoc. Or, heading south on the D2 from Cussac-Fort-Médoc, take the right-hand fork at Château Aney and follow signs to Château Maucaillou (*see* p.74) to reach Grand Poujeaux.

Returning to the Château Maucaillou, its arresting nineteenth-century château houses a museum of "The Vine and Wine Arts and Trade". The museum entrance fee includes a tour of the château and cellars, plus a tasting.

ABOVE *Reds from this part of the Médoc are said to smell of blackcurrants, cedar, cigar boxes, and pencil shavings.*

Around Listrac
The D5/E2 in front of Château Maucaillou leads, after 3km (2 miles) and via the hamlet of Medrac, to Listrac, which like Moulis has its own appellation. Listrac is traversed north-south by the busy N215/D1 Bordeaux-Lesparre road. The Maison du Vin et de Tourism de Listrac (*see* right) offers tasting of local wines, which change weekly, from June 1 to September 15. A small fee is payable. Listrac's best-sited vineyards lie around the town in an area called Le Fourcas, a name which features in the titles of several leading châteaux here. This is the highest area in the Médoc, at over 40m (130 feet) above sea level. Vineyards peter out to the west of the Listrac appellation, though here you will find Château Liouner, a winery which offers bed and breakfast accommodation amongst the tranquil Landes forests. Prices are average (Libardac, 33480 Listrac, tel: 05 56 58 05 62, liouner@aol.com).

Dynamic defender
Heading south from Listrac on the N215/D1 for 3km (2 miles) to Bouqueyran, turn right where Château Moulin-à-Vent and

LOCAL INFORMATION

Maison du Vin et de Tourism de Listrac
36 ave de Soulac
33480 Listrac
Tel: 05 56 58 09 56
vins.listrac@wanadoo.fr

Maison du Tourism de Moulis
1137 Le Bourg
33480 Moulis-en-Médoc
Tel: 05 56 58 32 74
châteaux@moulis.com
The Moulis tourist office provides free maps for those wishing to organise their own tours.

Château Mayne-Lalande (see p.74) are signposted. Bernard Lartigue is Listrac's most dynamic small producer and a passionate defender of Listrac in general and Bordeaux in particular. He founded Mayne-Lalande in 1992, having farmed cereal crops. Delicious Bordeaux Rosé and moreish Listrac reds are for short-to-medium term drinking. The Lartigues offer bed-and-breakfast accommodation.

Bed and breakfast is also offered at Château Cap-Léon-Veyrin in Donissan, 3.5 km (2 miles) from Listrac centre. Owned by the Meyre family for several generations, Cap-Léon-Veyrin's vineyards are well to the south of Donissan where the château, an attractive eighteenth-century manor, is located (tel: 05 56 58 07 28, capleonveyrin@aol.com).

Finally, you will return through Moulis-en-Médoc, the centre of the Moulis appellation, on your way back to Arcins.

Walking tours

The tourist office in Moulis has organised a 12km (7.5-mile) walking trail (chemin pédestre), which is open all the year and takes in many wineries and sights of interest, such as the Tiquetorte windmill, the (somewhat run-down) Raze fountain and Moulis-en-Medoc's Romanesque St-Saturnin church with its fortified tower. Guided tours for groups are possible. (See p.73.)

Listrac, Moulis, and Central Medoc wine facts

Moulis has fewer than 100 vineyard owners, producing between three and four million bottles of red each year, from 600ha of vines, making Moulis the Médoc's smallest appellation. Nearly half the growers take their grapes to neighbouring Listrac's cooperative.

Listrac also has under 100 vineyard owners, and sixty of them bottle their own wine. Listrac has 660ha of vines planted, and each year produces similar amounts of wine to Moulis.

The best Haut-Médoc vineyards in the villages of Arsac, Avensan, Lamarque, and Cussac, as well as those in the separate appellations of Moulis and Listrac further inland, produce a range of wine styles: lighter wines for early drinking from sandy soils, crunchier, more mouth-filling ones from clay, with the smoothest (and most expensive) coming from the best soil of all to be found here: well drained shingly gravel over a chalky sub-soil.

Margaux and the southern Médoc

Those coming to the Médoc for the first time hardly believe they are entering one of the world's most revered wine regions as they cross the semi-industrial, semi-agricultural landscape that separates greater Bordeaux from the southern Médoc. The journey through suburbs like Le Bouscat, Bruges, and Eysines to reach Blanquefort and the D2E or N215 is dusty and frustrating (for a better route, see below). Road signs are often sited so low as to be obscured by passing lorries. But, if you make it through then this part of the Médoc has some of Bordeaux's most beautiful châteaux, and most admired wines.

Drained by the Dutch

It seems hard to believe that what are now Bordeaux's northern suburbs were barely populated until the late seventeenth century when Dutch engineers drained the low-lying land here. Journeys between villages had to be undertaken by boat.

Today the southern Médoc wine villages of Macau, Ludon, Le Pian, Le Taillan, Parempuyre, and Blanquefort produce red wines under the appellation of Haut-Médoc. Further north are the five villages entitled to the Margaux appellation.

The best Margaux reds are supremely smooth and laden with intense flavours of red and black fruits. Worldwide demand for these wines has never been stronger, and they are priced accordingly. You can buy Margaux wines which appear relatively cheap, but most are pretty average, so try before you part with your money.

Getting there

By car from Bordeaux take either the N215 to Castelnau de Médoc (thirty minutes), then head east to Avensan and Margaux, or take the route via Blanquefort suggested below. If coming from the right bank across the Pont d'Aquitaine motorway suspension bridge, you can save time and avoid staying on the Rocade, the Bordeaux ring road, to reach the N215 or D2E. Instead, take the

LEFT *Red grapes in Bordeaux take on their dark colour from mid-August onwards.*

BELOW *For many, Château Margaux is the most impressive estate of the Médoc, both for its architecture and its wine.*

LOCAL INFORMATION

Syndicat d'Initiative
33460 Macau
Tel: 05 57 88 60 95
This tourist office in the centre of Macau can help arrange winery visits.

Maison du Vin de Margaux
Place La Trémoille
33460 Margaux
Tel: 05 57 88 70 82
syndicat.margaux@wanadoo.fr
Margaux's Maison du Vin provides free maps for those wishing to follow a designated walking route around some of the local vineyards.

BELOW *The thin topsoils and fine gravel of the Cantenac plateau brings elegance to wines like Château Margaux, Brane-Cantenac and Palmer.*

first exit coming off the Pont d'Aquitaine and immediately double-back on yourself to get onto the D2E. Follow the road through the large industrial park to do this (less than 500m/1,640 feet). From the Pont d'Aquitaine to Macau it is less than 20km (13 miles). The D2E runs north along the Garonne's left bank, passes the Blanquefort golf course on the left, and takes you through farmland and woods to Macau, joining the D2 just south of Cantenac.

By train to Margaux it is thirty to forty-five minutes from Gare St-Jean in Bordeaux. Or, if you're on the bus, take CITRAM Aquitaine buses from place des Quinconces in Bordeaux centre, destination Margaux.

Travelling around

We start on the Bordeaux ring road (the Rocade) and go to Blanquefort, Parempuyre, Ludon-Médoc, Macau, Cantenac, Issan, Margaux, Marsac, Soussans, Margaux, Arsac, Labarde, Le Pian-Médoc, and back to the ring road. Quite a long route (96km/60 miles), with quite a lot to see.

Blanquefort and Parempuyre

From the Rocade, follow signs north to Blanquefort (see p.80) on the D2E. Château Dillon (www.château-dillon.com) is run by students at the local viticultural school and the vineyard is home to a number of vine-training experiments.

From Blanquefort head to Parempuyre for Château Clément-Pichon (tel: 05 56 35 23 79, free daily visits by appointment). This nineteenth-century Gothic castle was restored by Clément Fayat, an industrialist who helped build many of Bordeaux's major roads.

Between Parempuyre and Ludon-Médoc to the north on the right-hand side of the D210 is the picture-perfect Château d'Agassac (tel: 05 57 88 15 47), a well-restored, moated château dating from the eleventh century and surrounded by vines and forest.

Entering the appellation

Stay on the D210 through the eastern part of Ludon-Médoc. On the left you go past Château d'Arche (www.châteaudarche.com) and, further on towards Macau, Château Maucamps (tel: 05 57 88 07 64). Follow signs on the right for Macau's little port on the Gironde, or continue north on the D210 to reach the Margaux appellation.

This begins in Labarde at Château Dauzac (tel: 05 57 88 32 10), which takes its name from Pétrus d'Auzac who was granted title to the estate by Richard the Lionheart (1157–99), via a deed preserved in the Tower of London. Just up the road from Dauzac is Château Siran (château.siran@ wanadoo.fr), with its park of cyclamens that are in flower from late August until early October. The road continues straight on towards Cantenac, becoming the D2.

Cantenac

The first two major Cantenac estates are Château Kirwan's homely eighteenth-century manorhouse (www.châteaukirwan.com) and the ivy-covered, former Benedictine monastery of Château Prieuré-Lichine (*see* p.81). Visitor-friendly, Prieuré-Lichine is open daily including public holidays, though a prior appointment is preferred. The chateau's small "vine garden" shows the differences between the main Bordeaux grape varieties.

Stay on the D2 to pass the mid-nineteenth-century Château Palmer (tel: 05 57 88 72 72), with its four towers and three flags: Dutch, French, and British to denote the nationality of its three merchant owners. In the early 1800s, it was owned by a General Charles Palmer who served under the Duke of Wellington, but was bankrupted in the 1840s by his love of women and his vineyards. The château was not built until 1856, in the turreted Renaissance-style also apparent at Château Pichon-Longueville-Baron in Pauillac (*see* picture p.56).

Margaux in Margaux

An easy detour east off the D2 takes you to Château d'Issan, a seventeenth-century moated building. Rejoin the D2 in the hamlet of Issan and the commune of Margaux. The First-Growth Château Margaux (*G3*; www.châteaumargaux.com; visits only by prior appointment) is reached by passing Château Maléscot St-Exupéry (tel: 05 57 88 97 20), named in part after

ABOVE *Oyster huts, supplying a Bordelais passion.*

BELOW RIGHT *The waxy coatings on the grapeskins – the bloom – are wild yeasts that can make the juice ferment spontaneously.*

CYCLE HIRE

Veloc Médoc
22 chemin de Benqueyre
33460 Cantenac
Tel: 05 56 58 22 22
Open July and August
9am–8pm. Closed on
Tuesdays from March
to December.

When hiring a bike, don't
forget to bring some ID and
cash for a deposit (€100
to 500 depending on the
bike), part of which can
be used for an insurance
policy, should you wish
to take one out.

the grandfather of the airman and writer, Antoine de St-Exupéry, a former owner. The current owners are one branch of the Zuger family, while another branch owns Château Marquis d'Alesme-Becker, the next major estate north of Maléscot on the D2 (tel: 05 57 88 70 27). Paintings and antique winemaking equipment are on show.

Around Soussans

Head towards Soussans, the most northerly commune in the Margaux appellation, for the contrasting wines of Château Labegorce (labegorce@château-labegorce.fr), obviously rich and oaky, and Château Labegorce-Zédé (tel: 05 57 88 71 31), lighter and more subtle.

From Soussans head south through Bessan and Richet to Château Lascombes (see p.81), which is Margaux's biggest vineyard owner with vines in all five communes in the Margaux appellation. The château has a battery of cement vats, raised off the ground so the young wines can be drained by gravity. Château Lascombes is open daily by prior appointment except May 1 and December 25 to January 1.

A Rauzan double act

Keeping the western side of the commune of Margaux on your left, follow signs to the two Rauzans – the underwhelming Rauzan-Gassies and the more polished Château Rauzan-Ségla (see p.81). Rauzan-Ségla boasts a sparkling cellar and inspiring wines, and has done since the 1994 purchase by the Wertheimer family, owners of Chanel and now also of Château Figeac in St-Emilion.

Turn right out of Rauzan-Ségla, right at the T-junction and left over the railway line and back into Cantenac to access Château Cantenac-Brown (tel: 05 57 88 81 81, infochato@cantenacbrown.com). With over 350 windows, Cantenac Brown is one of the weirder-looking Médoc châteaux, and was designed by an Englishman called John Lewis Brown, a nineteenth-century painter best-known for his depictions of animals.

Often overlooked
Turning right out of Cantenac-Brown, you continue to the critically underrated Château Brane-Cantenac (see p.81). In 1820 Baron Hector de Brane ("the Napoleon of the vines") sold what later became Château Mouton-Rothschild in Pauillac to concentrate on his Cantenac vineyard. Brane-Cantenac's last owner Lucien Lurton made easy-drinking wines. Lurton gave each of his ten children a château, and Brane is now run by his son Henri.

From Brane-Cantenac turn left, then left again after Benqueyre to reach Château d'Angludet (tel: 05 57 88 71 41, contact@château-angludet.fr). This property dates from 1300 and is now owned by the Sichel family, British co-owners of Château Palmer (see above).

From d'Angludet to Arsac
From d'Angludet head to Arsac via Château du Tertre (tel: 05 57 97 09 09). In Arsac, take signs to Macau, passing the excellent Château Monbrison (tel: 05 56 58 80 04; visits by appointment only) on the left on the way. The next estate on the left is the improving Château Giscours (tel: 05 57 97 09 09), whose Dutch owner also owns Château du Tertre.

From Giscours rejoin the D2 south, leaving the Margaux appellation for the Haut-Médoc. On the left are the recently renovated (and frost-prone) Château Cambon-La Pelouse (tel: 05 57 88 40 32, www.cambon-la-pelouse.com), then it's the Château Cantemerle, whose turreted castle happens to be hidden in a wooded park (tel: 05 57 97 02 82/84, cantemerle@cantemerle.com).

Continue on the D2 for Château La Lagune (tel: 05 57 88 44 07) on the right, or the more visitor-friendly Château Paloumey (D2; tel: 05 57 88 00 66, info@châteaupaloumey.com) on the left. Head south on the D2 towards Le Pian-Médoc for signs on the left to Château de Malleret (tel: 05 56 35 05

WHERE TO STAY AND EAT

BED AND BREAKFAST:
Domaine Marguy
46 chemin de Boulibranne
33460 Margaux
Tel: 05 57 88 36 71
malauryne@wanadoo.fr
No wineries in Margaux
offer b&b, but this one lies
in a protected 12-ha park.

HOTEL-RESTAURANTS:
Le Pont Bernet
33290 Le Pian-Médoc
Tel: 05 56 70 20 19
logifrance@pont-bernet.fr
Located opposite the Golf
du Médoc course (see
activities). Tennis, swimming
pool, plus gastronomic
restaurant.

Café-Restaurant-Hôtel
Les Landes
place Romain Videau
33480 Castelnau de Médoc
Tel: 05 56 58 73 80
Relaxed hotel-restaurant
offering snails Bordeaux-
style (in a wine, tomato
and ham sauce), scallops,
and roast lamb in garlic
butter. Restaurant closed
Sundays.

Hostellerie des Criquets
130 avenue du
11 Novembre
33290 Blanquefort
Tel: 05 56 35 09 24
hotel-des-criquets@
wanadoo.fr
The restaurant is open
at midday and for dinner,
but closed for Saturday
lunch, Sunday evening
and all day Monday.
Specialities include boned
pigeon, lobster, and
sturgeon in red
wine sauce.

36), a nineteenth-
century estate with
English stables.

From here the D2
takes you back to
Bordeaux centre via
the Rocade.

Other activities

Golf: Try Golf du
Médoc (chemin de
Courmateau Louens,
33290 Le Pian
Médoc, tel: 05 56
70 11 90, golf.du.
médoc@wanadoo.fr,
www. golf-du-médoc.com). This thirty-six-hole course hosted the
French Open in 1999. There's a golf school (and courses are
given in English as well as French) plus a restaurant.

Hôtel du Golf (Domaine de l'Ardilouse, 33680 Lacanau
Océan, tel: [hotel] 05 56 03 92 92, [golf] 05 56 03 92 98).
This eighteen-hole golf course has its own hotel, and is situated
midway between Lacanau's lake and the Atlantic. All-in packages
are available here, covering breakfast, lunch, evening meals,
accommodation, and green fees for an eighteen-hole round. Or,
if you prefer, you can have unlimited practice and simply pay for
time on the course by the hour.

Surfing: The nearest beaches from the south part of the
Médoc are at Lacanau-Océan on the Atlantic, or further inland
around Lacanau, on the Lac de Lacanau. Lacanau-Océan is a
regular venue for world surfing championship competitions. To
learn how to surf, contact Surf Plus (tel: 06 88 33 12 21,
www.lacanau-surf.com). Course fees include instructor, boards,
wetsuit, civil insurance and board wax, and there are full-time
(ten ninety-minute lessons) and part-time (five ninety-minute
lessons) courses. To get to the Lacanau region follow signs from
Castelnau de Médoc or Blanquefort. The journey takes less than
an hour (45–60km/30–40 miles).

Cycling and hiking: There is a designated 100km (62-
mile) cycle trail and hiking network through the pine forests
which separate Lacanau and Lacanau-Océan. These trails
incorporate the nature reserve at Cousseau, a pond forming
part of the larger Hourtin and Carcans lake, directly north of the
Lacanau lake.

For cycle hire try Locacycles, Avenue de l'Europe, 33680
Lacanau-Océan (tel: 05 56 26 30 99). Slightly further inland

and thus closer to the wine regions at Le Moutchic, a hamlet on the northern edge of Lacanau lake, is Moutchic Loisirs, Le Moutchic, 33680 Lacanau, tel: 05 56 26 22 43).

Horse riding: Try Domaine Aplus which caters for beginners and experienced riders (route Baganais, 33680 Lacanau-Océan, tel: 05 56 03 91 00 or info@aplus-lacanau.com or www.aplus-lacanau.com). You can bring your own horses, too. This is a hotel-restaurant, which also has small villas and apartments to rent. The stables form part of the hotel complex.

For more information on what Lacanau has to offer, have a look at www.lacanau.com, or contact the tourist office (tel: 05 56 03 21 01).

Margaux and southern Médoc wine facts

Margaux produces between eight and ten million bottles of red each year from around 1,400ha of vines in the communes of Cantenac, Labarde, Arsac, Soussans, and Margaux itself. Around sixty per cent of the vineyard land here belongs to twenty-one *grand cru* châteaux.

In 1855, these estates were classified: Châteaux Margaux (First Growth); Brane-Cantenac, Rauzan-Ségla, Rauzan-Gassies, Durfort-Vivens and Lascombes (Second Growths); Giscours, Kirwan, d'Issan, Malescot-St-Exupéry, Cantenac-Brown, Desmirail, Ferrière, Marquis d'Alesme-Becker, Boyd-Cantenac (Third Growths); Pouget, Prieuré-Lichine (Fourth Growths); Dauzac, du Tertre (Fifth Growths). There is also the Third-Growth Château La Lagune in the Haut-Médoc commune of Ludon, and the Fifth Growth Château Cantemerle in the commune of Macau.

Margaux has around eighty wineries, most of which produce a second and even a third wine as well as the main château wine. A typical wine is blended from Cabernet Sauvignon (fifty to sixty per cent) plus Merlot (forty to sixty per cent), Cabernet Franc and Petit Verdot (up to twenty per cent combined).

CHATEAUX IN MARGAUX

Château Brane-Cantenac
33460 Cantenac
Tel: 05 57 88 83 83 *(F2)*

Château Lascombes
33460 Margaux
Tel: 05 57 88 97 43 *(F3)*
châteaulascombe@wanadoo.fr

Château Prieuré-Lichine
36 ave de la 5ème
République, 33460 Cantenac
Tel: 05 57 88 36 28 *(F1)*
prieure.lichine@wanadoo.fr

Château Rauzan-Ségla
33460 Margaux
Tel: 05 57 88 82 10 *(F3)*

PRICES: expensive

LEFT *Menus often focus on the sea.*

BELOW *Spring is a particularly pleasant time to visit.*

Pessac-Léognan and Graves

The whole Graves region stretches 60km (40 miles) from the edge of the city of Bordeaux to Langon. The northern half is called Pessac-Léognan, after its two leading wine communes. This is where the most renowned châteaux are found, although they fight the urban sprawl for survival. To the south, landscape takes over from townscape, but the billboards advertising local garages and supermarkets still intrude on pine woods, pasture, and vineyard. This is the southern Graves, where wines are labelled simply "Graves".

ABOVE *Wherever you are in Bordeaux it seems water is never far away.*

RIGHT *Bordeaux's waterfront is one of France's most impressive. Warehouses running back from the Quai des Chartrons have been used to store wine in barrel and bottle since the mid-seventeenth century.*

Suburban vineyards

Bordeaux has vines on its doorstep, and used to have more until the city's growth swallowed them up. These city vineyards date from the Roman era, when the port was developed. After Bordeaux came under English control in the twelfth century the forests were cut back in order that vines could be planted. The region took its name, Graves, from the gravel soil.

Even the local archbishop, the future pope Clement V, was tempted to plant a vineyard here: Château Pape Clement (www.pape-clement.com) in Pessac. Close by is one of Bordeaux's finest properties, Château Haut-Brion (www.haut-brion.com), a green island in the suburbs, hidden from the Bordeaux-Madrid railway line in parts by a pre-fabricated concrete wall that is rarely graffiti-free.

Pepys and the "new French clarets"

Unlike the Médoc where red wines dominate almost to the exclusion of all else, Pessac-Léognan and Graves also produce dry white wines – arguably Bordeaux's best. But, it was what became known as "new French clarets" that gave this region and Bordeaux in general its fame. Indeed, the first known tasting note for a single-estate claret was written by the famous London diarist Samuel Pepys.

In 1663, he described wine from Château Haut-Brion as having the most "particular" taste he'd ever come across.

Perhaps Haut-Brion owed its success to its then owner, who was supposedly the first in Bordeaux to make sure his barrels were kept fully topped up, to stop the wines spoiling to vinegar. Pepys was served the wine at dinner in a London inn, and the region's reds have never lost their suitability as a match for food, as visitors to the city's top eateries will discover (see p.84).

Getting there

By car, there are the two main roads running the length of the Graves/Pessac-Léognan region, the A62 and the N113. The latter is the most suitable as the A62 only has three exits: at Beautiran/La Brède, Illats/Cérons and Langon. By train, take TER services from Bordeaux's Gare St-Jean in the direction of Langon. If booking on the SNCF website, make sure you specify Langon (33) in the Gironde region and not Langon (35) which is in Brittany. By bus, take Citram Aquitaine's Ligne 501 from Bordeaux for Langon, or Ligne 504 for Léognan.

Travelling around (see map p.87)

From Bordeaux city centre this route heads in a southeast direction, taking us to Cadaujac, detours to Léognan, back to Castres, Portets, Arbannats, Podensac, Barsac, Preignac, Langon, ending with Roaillon and Mazères. This route is roughly 48km (30 miles) in length, and if you drove around non-stop, it would take about ninety minutes.

LOCAL INFORMATION

Office du Tourisme
12 cours de XXX Juillet
33000 Bordeaux
Tel: 05 56 00 66 00
Can handle general tourist enquiries, as well as more wine-specific ones.

Office de Tourisme du Sauternais, Graves et Pays de Langon
11 allées Jean Jaurès
33210 Langon
Tel: 05 56 63 68 00
office-du-tourisme-langon@wanadoo.fr
One of Bordeaux's more helpful tourist offices.

WHERE TO EAT

Le Chapon Fin
5 rue Montesquieu
33000 Bordeaux
Tel: 05 56 79 10 10
Favourite eatery for
Bordeaux's wealthier
movers and shakers. Plush
decor matching epicurean
delights such as *foie gras
de canard confit* and lamb
stuffed with sage butter.

La Tupina
5 rue Porte de la Monnaie
33000 Bordeaux
Tel: 05 56 91 56 37
Well-chosen wine list
highlighting many good
lesser châteaux. Gascon-
style decor and menu, with
cooking on open fires.

L'Estaquade
quai Queyries
33000 Bordeaux
Tel: 05 57 54 02 50
Restaurant on a pier over
the Garonne on the right
bank (Bordeaux Bastide).
Cross the Pont de Pierre
from Bordeaux, turn left.

Cochon Volant
22 place des Capuchins
33000 Bordeaux
Tel: 05 57 59 10 00
Good pit-stop for late-night
steak and chips, catering
to the pre-club crowd.
Food service stops at 2am.
Near the Marché du
Capuchins, the major
produce market.

Restaurant L'Iguane
83 avenue JF Kennedy
33700 Mérignac
Tel: 05 56 34 07 39
Fish specialist on the
ground floor of the Quality
Suites hotel, which is found
by taking signs to "Centre
Hotelier" from Mérignac
airport. Closed Saturday
lunch and all day Sunday.

Bordeaux the city

Bordeaux likes to think of itself as France's second city (residents of Lyon disagree), but in wine terms no European city is as grand. Much of the city dates from the early nineteenth century, although the warehouses and cellars of the Quai des Chartrons, where wine was loaded onto boats waiting on the Gironde, date from the seventeenth.

As the city became rich on its wine and trade, architectural gems began to appear: the Grand Théatre and place de la Comédie from 1773, the allées de Tourny from 1745, the place de la Bourse from 1731, and the Place de Quinconces, the largest city square in Europe. Built from 1894, its central monument is to the Girondin revolutionaries; they took their name from that of the region, the Gironde. The Bordeaux Tourist Office (see p.83) can help organize a route around old Bordeaux where these sights, and more, are found.

Where to shop

For shopping, try the long rue Ste-Catherine, which runs from the Grand Théatre to the Place de la Victoire, which is also a good jumping-off point for the Graves and Pessac-Léognan vineyards to the south (*see* "Bordeaux to Bouscaut", below).

Rue Ste-Catherine can be a bit of a tourist trap, and is a magnet for pickpockets and people selling marijuana or hashish, with deals often concluded in the back streets around Place de la Victoire. For the more upmarket purchases try the area known as The Golden Triangle, formed by the Cours de l'Intendence, the Allées de Tourny, and Cours Georges Clemenceau. The streets inside the Golden Triangle, and the circular Grandes Hommes market in the centre of it are excellent for clothes and food; there are very good butchers and cheese shops here, and downstairs in the Grandes Hommes market there is a good supermarket: useful to remember for everyday practical needs.

Making the most of the markets

Pessac has two weekly markets in place de la République next to the *mairie*, one on Sunday mornings for general produce, and one on Tuesday mornings for organic produce. There are also organic markets on Thursday mornings on Bordeaux's quai Louis XV11 (St-Pierre), near the esplanade des Quinconces, and on Saturday mornings on the avenue St-Amand in the southwestern suburb of Caudéran.

For more information on organic farmers and growers in the Bordeaux region contact CIVAM BIO (7 le Grand Barrail, 33570 Montagne St-Emilion, tel: 05 57 74 03 25, civam.bio33@free.fr, www.civambio33.chez.tiscali.fr).

Night owls should visit Bordeaux's best-known market, the Marché des Capucins or the "belly of Bordeaux", sometimes nicknamed the "Capus" by the locals. This 300-year-old covered market takes place from Tuesday to Sunday, from midnight until around midday at place des Capucins (between pont de Pierre and cours de la Marne). Restaurateurs, chefs, café owners, and grocers have usually made their purchases by 4am, but activity picks up again with local residents stopping by on their way to work. Produce comes from all over France, and sometimes even further afield.

Bordeaux to Bouscaut

From the centre of Bordeaux get on the N113 Langon road. From Place de la Victoire follow the Cours de la Somme which

LEFT *The French are not afraid of being nosy, so get used to being stared at. At least this stone face has an excuse for not averting his gaze.*

BELOW *Cafés open early so as to be ready for people on their way to work.*

CHATEAUX IN PESSAC-LEOGNAN AND GRAVES
. . . .

Château Bouscaut
33140 Cadaujac
Tel: 05 57 83 12 20 *(C4)*
cb@chateau-bouscaut.com

Château Carbonnieux
33850 Léognan
Tel: 05 57 96 56 20 *(C4)*
www.carbonnieux.com
chateau.carbonnieux@
wanadoo.fr

Château Haut-Lagrange
31 rte de Loustalade
(D111)
33850 Léognan
Tel: 05 56 64 09 93 *(C4)*
chateau.haut-lagrange@
wanadoo.fr

Château Roquetaillade-la-Grange
33210 Mazères
Tel: 05 56 76 14 23 *(F2)*
www.roquetaillade.com
contact@roquetaillade.com

Château St-Hilaire
33640 Portets
Tel: 05 56 67 12 12 *(C4)*

Vieux-Château-Gaubert
33640 Portets
Tel: 05 56 67 18 63 *(C3)*
dominique.haverlan@
wanadoo.fr

PRICES: moderate to expensive

becomes the Route de Toulouse, then the N113 once you cross the A630 ring road.

In Cadaujac, turn right at the only traffic light in the direction of Léognan (route de Léognan), then turn immediately left, direction Martillac, and the first entrance on the left is Château Bouscaut (*see left*). The château had to be rebuilt in the 1960s when a steak grilling on vine shoots set light to the main building. The wines are soft, creamy, Sémillon-influenced dry whites and pleasantly peppery reds from a vineyard extending out from the château's terrace.

A taste of Benedictines
From Château Bouscaut take the route de Léognan, and 3km (2 miles) from Bouscaut, on the right-hand side, is Château Carbonnieux (*see left*). The double-turretted château with thirteenth-century origins was once inhabited by Benedictine monks. The current owners are the Perrins, who produce a large and reliable range.

From Château Carbonnieux, head to Léognan on the D111. In Léognan, take the D109 to La Brède and Martillac, and after 1–1.5km (around a mile) you will see Château Haut-Lagrange on the left, near the big roundabout (*see left*). In 1989, Francis Boutemy took over this vineyard, which had been abandoned since World War I. He drained it to reduce the risk of frost, and now makes warm, inviting, dry whites and reds.

Inky organics
From Château Haut-Lagrange, take the D109 to Martillac, turning left at Le Breyat to get back onto the N113, direction Langon. As you leave the south side of Castres on the N113, Château St-Hilaire is on the left (*see left*). This organic vineyard is run by the Guérin family. It produces good value, inky reds. At St-Hilaire there is also a *gîte* for rent (tel: 05 56 81 54 23).

From Château St-Hilaire, carry on to Portets for Vieux-Château-Gaubert (*see left*). It's the first château on the right after Château Rahoul has appeared on the left. At Vieux-Château-Gaubert Dominique Haverlan has made good use of the small vineyard his father gave him, expanding to produce a range of wines whose vivid fruitiness hints at New World opulence.

Getting to Langon
From Portets, carry on down the N113 for 24km (15 miles) to Langon. By this time you will have crossed the

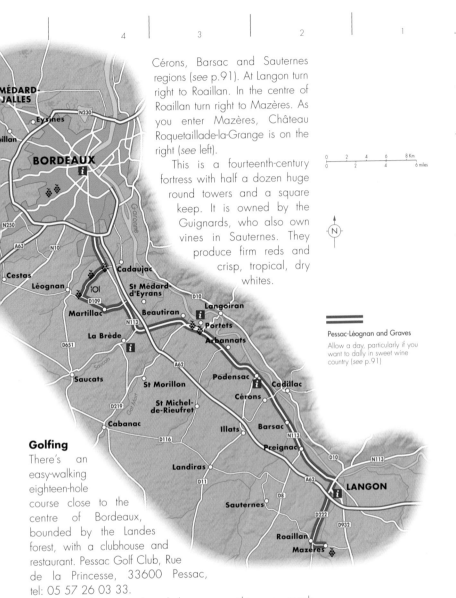

Cérons, Barsac and Sauternes regions (see p.91). At Langon turn right to Roaillan. In the centre of Roaillan turn right to Mazères. As you enter Mazères, Château Roquetaillade-la-Grange is on the right (see left).

This is a fourteenth-century fortress with half a dozen huge round towers and a square keep. It is owned by the Guignards, who also own vines in Sauternes. They produce firm reds and crisp, tropical, dry whites.

Pessac-Léognan and Graves

Allow a day, particularly if you want to dally in sweet wine country (see p.91)

Golfing

There's an easy-walking eighteen-hole course close to the centre of Bordeaux, bounded by the Landes forest, with a clubhouse and restaurant. Pessac Golf Club, Rue de la Princesse, 33600 Pessac, tel: 05 57 26 03 33.

There's also an eighteen-hole course within easy reach (5km/3 miles) of Langon. It's the Graves et Sauternais Golf Club, and is at St-Pardon-de-Conques, 33210 Langon, tel: 56 62 25 43.

Botanical garden

Bordeaux's fine botanical garden, the Jardin Botanique de Bordeaux, is on the right bank of the Garonne opposite the place des Quinconces (quai de Queyries, 33100 Bordeaux-Bastide, tel: 05 56 52 18 77, j.botanique@ mairie-bordeaux. fr) and is not to be missed. It contains tropical and medicinal

LEFT *Bordeaux is so obsessed by wine that even the city's airport has a small vineyard, planted with all the different grape varieties grown in the region.*

WHERE TO STAY

Le Burdigala
115 rue Georges-Bonnac
Tel: 05 56 90 16 16
burdigala@ burdigala.com
Luxury, modern,
international-style hotel
in downtown Bordeaux.

Hotel Claude Darroze
95 cours Général Leclerc
33210 Langon
Tel: 05 56 63 00 48
restaurant.darroze@
wanadoo.fr
Comfortable hotel with
very good restaurant
offering local specialities
like *salade landaise, foie
gras de canard, lamproie
au blanc de poireaux,*
and *agneau de Médoc à
l'estragon.* Terrace outside.

Hotel Normandie Bordeaux
7 cours XXX Juillet
33000 Bordeaux
Tel: 05 56 51 68 91
Centrally located (close
to the CIVB) and popular
with the wine trade for
its atmosphere.

Chalet Lyrique
169 cours du Gen
de Gaulle (RN10)
33170 Gradignan
Tel: 05 56 89 11 59
info@chalet-lyrique.fr
Easily located on the
Bordeaux-Biarritz road.
Closed July 29 to August
29. Comfortable rooms,
too, some recently
modernized.

Hotel La Bayonne
4 rue Martignac,
33000 Bordeaux
Tel: 05 56 48 00 88
Centrally located, quiet,
and comfortable. Swimming
pool and bar but no
restaurant.

plants brought from all over the world since the port's eighteenth-century heyday. Many of the plants to be seen here were grown and used for various medicinal purposes by the religious orders and apothecaries. Entry is free, and opening times are 8am–8pm in summer, and 8am–6pm in winter.

Finding out more about wine

The Conseil Interprofessionnel du Vin de Bordeaux provides free information on all fifty-seven wine-growing regions in Bordeaux (*see right*). The Syndicat d'Initiative des Graves de Montesquieu can help coordinate group tours of Château de la Brède, and local activities either side of the visit, too. The Maison des Vins de Graves can provide information on the Graves, Cérons, and Pessac-Léognan regions, and has wines for tasting and sale. There is plenty of space to park outside, and the staff are multilingual. They can help organize winery visits, too.

Where to buy wine

If you are looking for bargains, wine shops in Bordeaux are not the answer. They often have excellent ranges of smart wines, but they are catering to customers who are not particularly concerned about paying high prices.

Try big hypermarkets anywhere in France, especially in the run-up to autumn when wines from everyday châteaux and some of the lesser classed growths are put on *"premier prix"* or special offer. You will find some good wines in among the lesser examples if you know what you are looking for.

Having said that, one of Bordeaux's better wine shops, to be found not far from the offices of the Bordeaux Wine Bureau (CIVB), is called Le Magasin Intendant (2 Allée de Tourny, 33000 Bordeaux, tel: 05 56 48 01 29).

Don't miss this

Château La Brède is an arresting moated château with a thirteenth-century keep, this was the birthplace (1689) and home of the politician, writer and statesman Charles de Segondat, Baron de La Brède and de Montesquieu. It's a national historic monument, so it's open to the public at the beginning of September each year during the Journées de la Patrimoine ("Heritage Days"); (avenue du Château, 33650 La Brède, tel: 05 57 20 20 49).

Château La Brède hit the headlines in 1996 when its then incumbent, an elderly lady whose republican spirit deserted her momentarily, raised the drawbridge, leaving coachloads of would-be visitors perplexed on the wrong side of the moat.

Bordeaux wine history

Bordeaux's Chartrons district was where wine brokers and merchants established themselves, many coming from abroad to settle here from the mid-seventeenth century. They would blend wine to order and ship it abroad, and there is a museum that shows how this would have been done. Musée des Chartrons (41 rue Borie, 33300 Bordeaux, tel: 05 57 87 50 60, www.musee-des-chartrons.com).

There's also a tastefully decorated wine museum in a former merchant's cellar charting Bordeaux's journey from Roman times.

LEFT *The Pont d'Aquitaine opened in 1967 and is nearly a mile long. Avoid rush hour when traffic clogs up from the ring road. Another bridge, further north, is being planned.*

Audio commentaries are available in French, English, German, Spanish, Italian, and Japanese. (Vinorama, 12 cours du Médoc, 33000 Bordeaux, tel: 05 56 39 39 20.)

LUXURY SPA

. . . .

Sources de Caudalie
chemin de Smith-Haut-Lafitte
33650 Martillac
Tel: 05 57 83 83 83
sources@sources-caudalie.com
Part of Château-Smith-Haut-Lafitte. Treatments here feature grape extracts in various forms. The buildings are modern, but have been made using old timbers. There's a hotel and two restaurants (closed Mondays and Tuesdays): the gourmet La Grand Vigne (inspired by France's eighteenth-century orangeries), and the inn-style La Table du Lavoir (a room that was once a laundry/wash house for grape-pickers).

Pessac-Léognan and Graves wine facts
Today, the Graves region is divided into two parts: Pessac-Léognan in the north, and Graves in the south. Pessac-Léognan produces around seven million bottles of exuberant wines from 1,250ha of red vines and 250ha of white. Graves produces around twenty million bottles of bold, ageable wine from 2,600ha of red vines and 1,100ha of white.

The reds are typically made from up to sixty per cent Cabernet Sauvignon and thirty per cent Merlot, plus Cabernet Franc, Malbec, and Petit Verdot. They show lovely brick-red colours and ripe plum-skin textures: juicy but firm.

The grape mix for white wines is more varied, with some châteaux, such as Château Couhins-Lurton (andre.lurton@andrelurton.com) favouring Sauvignon Blanc, while others, such as Château Laville-Haut-Brion (www.laville-haut-brion.com) are more Sémillon-oriented. Sweetish whites under the Graves Supérieures appellation can be headachey.

Cérons, Sauternes, and Barsac

The little river Ciron is barely noticeable to anyone passing it on the road. Yet the Ciron helps create Bordeaux's world-renowned sweet white wines: when its cool waters meet those of the warmer, tidally influenced Garonne, low-lying mists form to shroud the vineyards. These mists encourage the spores of a fungus called *Botrytis cinerea*. When the fungus settles on ripe grapes it causes them to shrivel, becoming sweeter and more concentrated. The result is sweet, golden wines, and another name for the fungus – noble rot.

How did it begin?

No one is quite sure when the first sweet botrytized white wines were produced in the Sauternes region, although white wines have been made here for hundreds of years. Muscat grapes were grown in the sixteenth and seventeenth centuries to imitate the sweet wines from Spain that were then fashionable, but they were made in a very different way from today's Sauternes. Gradually Sémillon, Sauvignon Blanc, and Muscadelle were planted, and sometimes picked extra-late for extra-rich wines. But late picking was costly, and risked losing the crop to bad late autumn weather.

Presidential election

In 1787, America's Ambassador to France (and future President) Thomas Jefferson visited the region. He described Sauternes as one of the best wines in the country.

He ordered ten dozen bottles of Yquem, later introducing the wine to his friend George Washington, who asked for thirty dozen, and although we know from descriptions of the time that the wine was "stronger" than other contemporary white wines no one can say for sure how sweet it tasted, if indeed it was sweet at all.

Russian revolution

It was possibly only after 1859 that the sweetness for which Sauternes would become famed became popular among wine producers in the region. The brother of the then Russian Tsar paid huge sums for the 1847 Yquem which had been picked late

LEFT *Château La Mission Haut-Brion formed part of Haut-Brion until 1630 when it passed to a holy order who created its small chapel ("mission").*

BELOW *The Ciron rises in the Landes forest.*

SERVING SWEET WHITE BORDEAUX

For sweet white wines the rule is: the **better the bottle the less chilled** it needs to be. Overchilling bottles deadens the flavours.

It is rare in Bordeaux to serve sweet white wines with desserts like chocolate or iced cream. Instead, the **locals contrast the wine's sweetness** by serving it with savoury dishes like *pâté de foie gras* and **salad** as a starter, or with cheese (especially **blue cheese**), nuts and dried or fresh fruit at the end of a meal.

Typical main course options in local restaurants include chicken (*poulet*), quail (*caille*), and bunting (*ortolan*), or turbot (*turbot*), sole (*sole*), and quenelles of pike (*brochet*).

BELOW *A reminder of more troubled times – a lookout tower in defensive walls.*

and made from nobly rotten grapes. The style caught on at the Russian court, and the popularity of Sauternes as we know it was established.

Getting there

By car from the Bordeaux ring road it is 40km (25 miles) to Langon a few kilometres south of Preignac. The journey takes less than an hour on the route de Toulouse or RN113 (from exit 18), or the E72/A62 motorway (from exit 19), direction Langon-Agen-Toulouse.

Trains from Bordeaux St-Jean stop at Podensac (fifteen minutes), Cérons (twenty minutes), Barsac (twenty-five minutes), and Preignac (thirty minutes).

By bus, take Citram Aquitaine's Ligne 501 from Bordeaux to Langon from Place des Quinconces in Bordeaux city centre.

Travelling around

To make the most of this unique area, we have two routes. Route One goes to Cérons and is roughly 19km (12 miles), and would take less than an hour with no stops. This takes us from Podensac to Illats and Cérons.

Route two covers Barsac and Sauternes and is about 48km (30 miles) in length. This slightly longer trip takes us from Barsac to la Peloue and Le Haire, then Boutoc, Bommes, Sauternes, Fargues, Preignac, and back to Barsac.

Route one: apéritif in Podensac

Cérons can be made in three communes: they are Podensac, Illats, and Cérons itself. Podensac has no stand-out winery but is home to the Maison des Vins de Graves (*see* p.89) and the producers of the apéritif Lillet (*see* p.94).

The firm of Lillet was founded in 1872 by brothers Raymond and Paul Lillet. Their eponymous drink is a sweetish blend of red or white wine, brandy, fruits, and herbs. White Lillet is usually served on ice with lime, red Lillet with orange peel.

Visits to the stills and oak-ageing vats can take place between 9.30am and 6pm on weekdays and Saturdays from June 15 to September 15.

Around Illats

The journey to sleepy Illats on the D11 traverses first farmland and then, from the hamlet of Barrouil, the Landes pine forests. The commune takes its name from a hill (*hillot*) of fine red gravel upon which the finest vineyards, those of Château Hillot (tel: 05 56 62 53 38), sit.

Take the D117E from Illats back to Cérons and the well-signposted Château du Seuil (*see* p.94). It is named after the *sill* or crossing which horses could use to traverse the river

Garonne at low tide during Gallo-Roman times. It produces reliable red, white and sweet wines and is owned by the Welsh-Kiwi Allison family.

Cérons is where the three communes making up the Cérons appellation conjoin on the Plateau du Moulin-à-Vent, where the rival domaines of the Grand Enclos du Château de Cérons (tel: 05 56 27 01 53) and the Château de Cérons (tel: 05 56 27 01 13) have vineyards. They were part of the same domaine until they split in the mid-nineteenth century.

From Cérons head back to Bordeaux via Podensac on the RN113 road.

Route two: around Barsac and Sauternes

Getting around Barsac and Sauternes can be frustrating for two reasons. First, it can be hard to get one's bearings as vineyards are often surrounded by high stone walls.

Second, the barriers of the railway line, the Bordeaux-Toulouse motorway (A62), and the river Ciron mean you must plan your route carefully

Route one: Cerons
Half a day should suffice, so why not do together with...

Route two: Barsac and Sauternes
A day or two if you want to really get to know the area

RIGHT *Wine barrels end their days either as firewood or, more decoratively, as planters.*

if you are not to waste time doubling back on yourself for suitable crossing points.

Elegant Barsac

The most northerly commune in the Sauternes region, Barsac, is said to produce the most elegant wines. Its vineyards date from Roman times, as ruins from a Roman villa near the church have shown. Barsac's best wines come from the plateau southwest of the village.

On the edge of this plateau lies Château St-Marc (*see* left). To get there, follow signs to St-Marc from the nearby Barsac railway station. Take the D118 from Barsac and turn right immediately after the railway line, then first left. At Château St-Marc, Didier Laulan favours careful use of oak in his elegant sweet whites, and above-average percentages of Muscadelle; some of the Muscadelle vines date from 1910. Laulan also owns the Second Growth Château Broustet.

Doisy trio

From Château St-Marc follow the D118 past the recently replanted but inconsistent Château de Myrat (tel: 05 56 27 15 06), following signs to the hamlet of La Pelouse. Located here are the consistently excellent Château Coutet (www.château-coutet.com) and two of the three Doisys: the technologically brilliant Doisy-Daëne (tel: 05 56 27 15 84, doisy-daene@terre-net.fr) and the organic Doisy-Dubroca (info@louis.lurton.fr). To reach the other Doisy, Doisy-Védrines (tel: 05 56 27 15 13), continue past Château Piada and turn right onto the D114.

Yquem: greatest of the great

Continue on the D114 for just under a kilometre (half a mile) turning left onto the D109 and crossing the Ciron to reach the now-divided Château du Mayne. Instead of continuing on the D109 to the little town of Preignac, bear right past Château

CHATEAUX IN CERONS, SAUTERNES, AND BARSAC

Lillet
33720 Podensac
Tel: 05 56 27 41 44 *(F2)*
www.lillet.fr

Château de Malle
33210 Preignac
Tel: 05 56 62 36 86 *(C1)*
contact@château-de-malle.fr

Domaine du Rousset-Peyraguey
33210 Preignac
Tel: 05 56 63 49 43 *(B2)*
rousset.peyraguet@
wanadoo.fr

Château du Seuil
33720 Cérons
Tel: 05 56 27 11 56 *(F2)*
www.châteauduseuil.com
château-du-seuil@
wanadoo.fr

Château St-Marc
33720 Barsac
Tel: 05 56 27 16 87 *(E2)*
d.l.d@wanadoo.fr

PRICES: moderate to expensive

Haut-Bergeron (haut-bergeron@wanadoo.fr) through the hamlet of Le Haire. In front of you on a hill is Château d'Yquem (www.yquem.fr), for many the source of France's greatest sweet white wine. Yquem was in the hands of the same family from 1785 until 1997 when it became part of LVMH (Louis Vuitton-Moët Hennessey), the luxury goods group.

On the left is Château Suduiraut (tel: 05 56 63 27 29), a seventeenth-century château producing lush, oaky wines with a park designed by Le Nôtre, the landscape architect who created the gardens at the Palace of Versailles.

Jewels of Bommes
Just before the hamlet of Boutoc turn right onto the D116. When this becomes the D116E1 you are within the vineyards of Bommes, said to produce the Sauternes region's softest, lightest wines. Bommes is also home to the region's oldest château, the imposing thirteenth-century fortress of Château Lafaurie-Peyraguey (tel: 05 56 76 60 54), owned by the merchant Cordier.

Almost behind is Château Rayne-Vigneau (tel: 05 56 76 61 63) whose vineyard topsoils are said to contain precious stones like topaz, amethyst, and sapphires.

Ruins of Fargues
Turn right off the D116E1 onto the D125 and it is about 1.6km (1 mile) to the centre of the Sauternes commune. A kilometre past the town turn right for Château Filhot (www.filhot.com), an improving estate backing onto woodland with English-style gardens and an elegant early eighteenth-century château. Follow signs to Fargues on the D125, 3km (2 miles) away. The village is dominated by the ruins of Château de Fargues (www.château-de-fargues.com), owned by the former proprietors of Yquem, the Lur-Saluces family.

From Fargues follow signs to Château Rieussec (tel: 05 56 62 20 71), off the D8. In the 1920s this vineyard sometimes produced the better wine, and some think it could still. The estate (there is no château as such) is owned by the Rothschilds of Château Lafite in Pauillac.

Wine and lunar cycles
Leaving Rieussec turn right, and then right again at the first crossroads on the D8E4, direction Preignac. After 1.6km (1 mile) on the left are the distinctive vineyards of Domaine du Rousset-Peyraguey (see left). Alain Dejean is the Sauternes region's most environmentally aware grower. He farms 6ha of vines Biodynamically, spraying herbal infusions and so on onto the vines according to lunar cycles, and he makes diverting wine.

WHERE TO EAT

Braises et Gourmandises
18 rue de la Liberté
33210 Preignac
Tel: 05 56 62 30 58
Braises means "hot coals" or "embers". Grilled meat and locally caught fish are the specialities on this menu.

Restaurant du Cap Horn
33210 Preignac
Tel: 05 56 63 27 38
The Cap Horn overlooks the Garonne 100m from the RN113. The basic set menu is good value. Owner M Laffargue's Bazas beef grilled on vine prunings is recommended.

Auberge les Vignes
21 rue Principale
33210 Sauternes
Tel: 05 56 76 60 06
Hearty cooking from the Bialasik family, owners here since 1964, in a cosy restaurant opposite the church.

Le Saprien
33210 Sauternes
Tel: 05 56 76 80 87
Le Saprien's cooking is designed to match, rather than compete with Sauternes. There's a terrace overlooking the vines. The wine list has an extensive range of Sauternes available by the glass.

LOCAL INFORMATION

Office de Tourisme Sauternes
11 rue Principale
33210 Sauternes
Tel: 05 56 76 69 13
sauternes@wanadoo.fr
Can arrange winery visits or organize bicycle hire for those wishing to cycle around the vineyards.

Maison de Barsac
Place de l'Eglise
33210 Barsac
Tel: 05 56 27 15 44
Run by local wine-growers. Tourist information and wine sales.

Maison du Sauternes
14 Place de la Mairie,
33210 Sauternes
Tel: 05 56 76 69 83
Wine shop with reasonable selection of local wines.

See round a château

Continue on the D8E4, direction Preignac, crossing the A62 motorway, and take the first right to Château de Malle (*see* p.94). This dramatic, early-seventeenth-century château with its expansive gardens is the only national historic monument in Sauternes. It is open to visitors from Easter to mid-October. Solid dry white, red and sweet white wines are produced. From Château de Malle rejoin the D8E4 to reach Preignac, and when you get to Preignac take the N113 north for Barsac, heading towards Bordeaux.

Other activities

Club de Canoe Kayac Bommes Nautique organizes canoe trips down the river Ciron, which can last two days (15–20km/9–12.5 miles maximum) or just one (8–10km/5–6 miles), according to choice. Overnight stays can involve camping or staying in bed and breakfast accommodation, depending on the group. The club is located next to Château Lamourette at Base de Nautique (Le Tachon, 33210 Bommes, tel: 05 56 76 61 42).

Buying sweeties

Prices for even the most sought-after sweet white Bordeaux wines still offer relatively good value, compared to the stratospheric prices achieved at auction for Bordeaux's top red wines. One leading proprietor reckons that Sauternes prices ought to be double what they are – but, he says wistfully, even half as much again would be nice. When one remembers that there are years when no Sauternes or Barsac can be made at all, one cannot help but sympathize with his point of view. But these relatively low prices are to the advantage of consumers. Winemaking standards have improved greatly in recent years, even though prices have not risen much, and at the lower end of the market there are some well-made, good-value wines in Cérons and Barsac if you are prepared to hunt.

Research your vintages, though. There are years, like 1990, in which it was almost impossible to make poor wine, and all the wines are rich and luscious, but these years are rare. More common are years when rain interrupts the harvest, or when there just isn't much botrytis. Wines can vary then from light and semi-sweet (though certainly enjoyable, especially as apéritifs or with food) to sweet but without the true flavours of noble rot. Even the best châteaux need luck with the weather to make really successful wine. Don't despise off-vintages, though. A good winemaker can turn out better wine in a dodgy year than a bad winemaker might in a good one. Find a property you like, and trust it.

Cérons, Sauternes, and Barsac wine facts
Production of sweet white wines from Cérons, Barsac and Sauternes varies greatly from year to year, depending on whether noble rot (*Botrytis cinerea*) forms, with less than two million bottles being made in bad years and up to ten million in good ones. The harvest in Sauternes can last from September to November and even beyond, something to bear in mind when planning winery visits. Grape-pickers moving through the vines in a late autumn mist is one of the most atmospheric sights in Bordeaux.

Around 270 producers make sweet white wines in this part of Bordeaux. There is no local cooperative, but bulk wines are traded by merchants to the south in the town of Langon (*see* Graves and Pessac-Léognan p.82). A typical wine is blended from Sémillon (around eighty per cent) plus Sauvignon Blanc and Muscadelle (twenty per cent combined). A 125-centilitre glass of Cérons, Barsac or Sauternes contains approximately twenty-five grams of sugar.

Aside from the sweet wines, dry white and red wines are produced in Cérons and Barsac-Sauternes, and have the Graves appellation.

BELOW *Château d'Yquem was constructed as a medieval fortress and affords superb views over the Sauternes region.*

Bourg and Blaye

B laye and Bourg's vineyards are the first you encounter when arriving in Bordeaux by car or train from Paris and the north. In the Blaye region, vineyards surrounding the town of Blaye are widely scattered across rolling farmland, interspersed by woodland, meadow and, near the Gironde, marsh. Little streams called *esteys* running into the Gironde are home to baby eels, much prized as a delicacy by local restaurateurs.

Southerly Bourg

The Bourg region to the south is much more compact, and produces denser wines than Blaye. Historically, Bourg's reds were used by Bordeaux merchants to beef up their weedier Médocs, but Bourg is now establishing a reputation of its own for good-value reds with an agreeably mouth-coating quality.

Bourg's exploitation by the Médoc dates from the mid-nineteenth century, when Bordeaux wines began to be shipped by railway. These rendered Bourg's intricate system of waterways, geared to purely local supply, superfluous, and Bourg was left behind in the race for markets. As Médoc got more expensive in the boom years of the 1980s and 1990s, Bourg's red wines were increasingly seen as a good, less expensive alternative, especially if one's taste is for full reds with a crisp, generous bite.

RIGHT *Hand-picking is the exception here – most vines are machine-harvested.*

BELOW *Vines generally grow higher and more widely spaced on the Right Bank; soils are more fertile here.*

Getting there

By boat, you can take the ferry from Lamarque in the Médoc to Blaye to avoid the hassle of circumnavigating the city of Bordeaux (*see Margaux and the southern Médoc p.75* for details of the ferry).

By road, take the A10 Bordeaux-Paris motorway which is toll-free as far as St-André-de-Cubzac, and then the D669 to Bourg (which should take about forty minutes), or the N137 to Blaye (about one hour).

Travelling around

Because these two regions cover quite a large area, we have two routes for each appellation (*see* map p.100).

Bourg route one: approximately 24km (15 miles) in length, this starts in Bourg and goes to Tauriac, Pugnac, Lansac, and back to Bourg.

Bourg route two: about 32km (20 miles), this again starts in Bourg, but this time goes to Bayon, Comps, St-Ciers-de-Canesse, Plassac, Villeneuve, Bayon, and Bourg.

Blaye route one: roughly 26km (16 miles) long, we start in Blaye and go to Anglade, St-Seurin-de-Cursac, St-Paul-de-Blaye, and back to Blaye.

Blaye route two: about 66km (42 miles in length), we go from Blaye out east to Cubnezais and back to Blaye.

Bourg route one: a local snapshot

From the centre of Bourg, take the D669 to Prignac et Marcamps (*see* "local history" p.102). Turn left at the Cave de Bourg Tauriac cooperative onto the D133 to Tauriac. In Tauriac, take the D249 to Pugnac, and after 1km (0.6 mile) Château Haut-Macô (*see* p.103) appears. This is a visitor-friendly estate with quiet tasting room overlooking the semi-circular, air-conditioned barrel cellar. You can taste firm, Cabernet Sauvignon-dominated reds.

From Château Haut-Macô turn left where the D249 joins the N137, then left again after a few hundred metres to Lansac on the D23. After just over one mile Château Nodoz appears (*see* p.103). Brothers Jean-Louis and André Magdeleine produce two main wine labels at Nodoz: the white one offers value for early drinking, while the yellow one can age for up to twelve years. From here continue on the D23 to Bourg, stopping to admire the view from the Grand Puy hill in Lansac.

Bourg route two: the beauty of Biodynamics

From Bourg, take the D669E1 running northwest along the Gironde to Bayon. In Bayon, take the D133E7 going inland, direction Samonac. Château Falfas appears on the right after around 2km (1.3 miles); (*see* p.103). You should easily be able to spot the Falfas vineyards for alternate rows are turned by plough, and left for weeds and native flowers. Château Falfas practises Biodynamic viticulture.

Based on the teachings of Rudolf Steiner, Biodynamics is concerned with farming according to the movement of the moon and planets in relation to the Earth and the twelve astronomical constellations of the zodiac. Instead of commonly used weedkillers and fertilisers, wines are treated with remedies based on minute quantities of plants, minerals, and animal manures. The estate has been Biodynamic since 1988. Its

LOCAL INFORMATION

Office du Tourisme
Hôtel de la Jurade
4 place de la Liberation
33710 Bourg-sur-Gironde
Tel: 05 57 68 31 76

Office du Tourisme
2 allées Marines
33710 Blaye
Tel: 05 57 42 12 09

**Maison du Vin des
Côtes de Bourg**
1 place de l'Eperon
33710 Bourg-sur-Gironde
Tel: 05 57 94 80 20
www.cotes-de-bourg.com
info@cotes-de-bourg.com

**Maison du Vin des
Premières Côtes de Blaye**
11 cours Vauban
33390 Blaye
Tel: 05 57 42 91 19
www.premieres-cotes-blaye.com
contact@premieres-cotes-blaye.com
A selection of local wines are offered for tasting; you can also buy wines here.

winemaking is traditional, and uses stone vats and wooden basket-presses. There are bright, refreshing reds produced from fifty per cent Merlot, plus Cabernet Sauvignon (twenty-five per cent), Malbec, and Cabernet Franc.

Continue on the D133E7, turning left to Comps. In Comps pick up the D133 to St-Ciers-de-Canesse where Château de Repimplet (4 Repimplet, 33710 St-Ciers-de-Canesse) is a leading estate. Château de Repimplet's soils are full of deep red clay, mixed with gravel which gives the red wines notably deep colours and a refreshing crispness. Patrick Touret bought the château in 1986, since when he has resurrected it. His best red is named after his children, Amélie and Julien. Merlot gives Touret's wines their juicy, immediate appeal.

Château la Grolet is on the northwestern outskirts of St-Ciers-de-Canesse (see p.103). This is another Biodynamic Bourg domaine, producing rich, soft reds from seventy per cent Merlot, plus Cabernet Sauvignon and a dash of Cabernet Franc. Owners Catherine and Jean-Luc Hubert also own the organic Château Peybonhomme-les-Tours (peybonhomme@ terre-net.fr) in the Blaye region. La Grolet's château dates from the seventeenth century.

Vineyards in St-Ciers-de-Canesse are rarely affected by frost, keeping yields steady enough to maintain competitive prices.

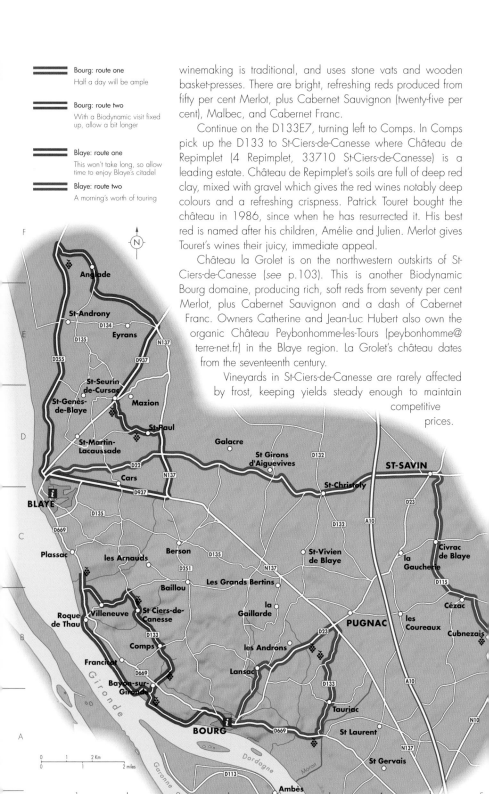

Bourg: route one
Half a day will be ample

Bourg: route two
With a Biodynamic visit fixed up, allow a bit longer

Blaye: route one
This won't take long, so allow time to enjoy Blaye's citadel

Blaye: route two
A morning's worth of touring

From Château la Grolet continue on the D133 for 0.5km, turning left to Villeneuve de Blaye and then on to Plassac on the coast road (the D669).

Château Haut-Mondésir – the wine is Merlot-dominated – lies on the border between the Bourg and Blaye regions, on the right-hand side of the D669 (see p.103). Marc and Laurence Pasquet own both this and the larger, machine-picked Château Mondésir-Gazin in the Blayais. They are a good starting place to learning how wines grown only a few metres apart can taste very different.

Return to Bourg along the D669 and D669E1 via Bayon. There is a good view across the Gironde to the Médoc in front of Château Eyquem on the eastern side of Bayon.

Blaye route one: gentle whites and rousing reds

From Blaye, take the D255 north through St-Genès-de-Blaye, then to St-Androny and on to Anglade, a journey of just under 11km (7 miles).

Château La Raz-Caman is signposted on the right at Caman. Jean-François Pommeraud produces gentle whites and occasionally fiery reds offering excellent value. Open daily all year except August, September, and October, and weekends; see p.103.

From here, take the D9E through Anglade towards the hamlet of Le Pontet northeast of Eyrans, to pick up the D937 south to Blaye. After 4km (2.5 miles) Château Roland la Garde is on the right at La Garde, just after the sign indicating a right turn to the commune of St-Seurin-de-Cursac. Bruno Martin's winery offers solid, Merlot-dominated reds and a collection of tastefully displayed, 50,000-year-old stone age relics. Open all year, daily, except Sundays (see p.103.)

Around St-Paul-de-Blaye

Take the windy D137 to St-Paul-de-Blaye. Just before you reach the centre of the commune, turn right for Courgeau where Château Les Jonqueyres is located. Pascal Montaut inherited this estate in 1978, but drank most of the cellar when he lived in a hippy commune.

Now, with his wife Isabelle, Montaut is regarded as one of Blaye's best winemakers for concentrated, Merlot-dominated reds. Open daily except Saturday afternoons, Sundays, and during October (see p.103).

Head back to Blaye by going east through St-Paul-de-Blaye, then turn right onto the N137 to head south for around 3km (2 miles) to pick up the D937 Blaye-St-André-de-Cubzac road. If you turn right it is 6km (4 miles) to Blaye. If you turn left it is 20km (12.5 miles) to St-André-de-Cubzac, beyond which is the Fronsac region (see p.104).

WHERE TO STAY

Hotel Les Trois Lis
11 place Libération
33710 Bourg-sur-Gironde
Tel: 05 57 68 22 86
Not overpriced, this has only basic creature comforts, but is centrally located.

Hotel Bellevue
2 cours Gen de Gaulle
33390 Blaye
Tel: 05 57 42 00 36
Medium-priced, no-frills accommodation plus simple restaurant.

Hotel-Restaurant La Citadelle
5 place Armes, 33390 Blaye
Tel: 05 57 42 17 10
Heading towards the luxury category, a modern hotel in Blaye's citadel with views of the Gironde. Swimming pool.

EATING OUT

. . . .

L'Hippocampe
3 rue 4 Septembre
33710 Bourg-sur-Gironde
Tel: 05 57 68 37 00
Fish restaurant with good
wine list.

Le Plaisance
Au Port de Bourg
33710 Bourg-sur-Gironde
Tel: 05 57 68 45 34
Part brasserie/pizzeria, part
gastronomic restaurant, this
overlooks the Gironde near
one of the three old fortified
gateways to old Bourg.

Le Troque Sel
1 place Jeantet
33710 Bourg-sur-Gironde
Tel: 05 57 68 30 67
Known for grilled meat.

Restaurant Le Petit Port
3 cours Port
33390 Blaye
Tel: 05 57 42 99 95
Popular with locals during
the week, and with
tourists seeking fresh fish
at weekends.

Restaurant Le Preymayac
27 rue Premayac
33390 Blaye
Tel: 05 57 42 19 57
Grilled meats and eels are
the attractions here.

Blaye route two: scenic jaunt

From the centre of Blaye, take the D22 east as far as St-Savin, a distance of 20km (12.5 miles). From St-Savin take the D115 to Civrac-de-Blaye, and then Cezac, to reach Cubnezais where Château Haut-Bertinerie (see right) is signposted, around 13km (8 miles) from St-Savin. This property is a fine source of reds, dry whites, and deep pink (clairet) wines grown on lyre-trained vines by the Bantegnies family.

Visitors can usually taste the same wine from several different vintages. Visits are by appointment. Return to Blaye by the scenic route by which you arrived, or more quickly by joining the N10 to just north of St-André-de-Cubzac (8km/5 miles), then turning right onto the D937 for Blaye (26km/16 miles).

Local history

Both Bourg and Blaye have medieval fortified citadels, built to protect locals from sea-borne attack. Blaye's citadel is the more impressive of the two, and dates from 1689. It contains an entire small village, with flower-decked streets and a hotel. Ask at the Blaye tourist office for a map (see p.99).

Also well worth a visit is the Museum of Prehistory in Prignac et Marcamps. The walls of the Pair-non-Pair cave are decorated with 30,000-year-old pictures of ibex, bulls, mammoths, and rhinoceros; access is via the D133. Visits are throughout the day at set times (they are usually no more than ninety minutes' apart) and it's best to reserve ahead by calling first (2 chemin Pair-Non-Pairtel, tel: 05 57 68 33 40, the museum is closed every Monday).

Pruning for quality

One potential clue as to wine quality in the vineyards of Bourg and Blaye is how the vines are pruned. You can best see this from spring to early summer, when the wines are stumps with little new leaf and shoot growth.

Vines are pruned to either cordons or canes. How do you tell the difference? Alll vines have a vertical trunk, but those pruned to cordons also have one or two thick, trunk-like horizontal arms coming out either side of the crown, or top, of the vine. Vines pruned to canes (like the ones in the photo on p.98) do not have these thick horizontal arms, but thinner, one-year-old canes or "baguettes" which look like the French bread sticks of that name.

Generally, growers in this part of Bordeaux pruning vines to cordons are looking to produce the maximum yield of grapes allowed under French appellation contrôlée rules, which still allow generous surpluses, too. The more quality-oriented growers generally prune to canes.

LEFT *The wines of Bourg have deep colour, from the grapes grown on the region's red clay soils.*

Bourg wine facts

The Bourg region covers 4,000ha of mainly red vines, with Merlot the dominant grape. Around twenty-five million bottles are produced each year. Cooperatives play an important part, but are less dominant here than in Blaye.

Bourg's vineyards mostly lie on sometimes surprisingly steep hills overlooking the Gironde, on red clay over limestone. The clay gives Bourg's reds their deep colour, while the limestone imparts freshness. Limestone was first quarried here by the Romans. From the late 1700s it was used to build many of the houses not just in Bourg but across the water in Bordeaux as well. The merchants' houses and warehouses that line the Quai des Chartrons, most of which have been cleaned in the last few years to reveal the beautiful colour of the stone, are often built of this so-called "plassac limestone".

Blaye wine facts

The Blaye region has around 6,000ha of vines, mainly Merlot, Cabernet Sauvignon, Malbec, and Cabernet Franc. Around forty million bottles are produced under the Blaye, Côtes de Blaye, and the increasingly popular Premières Côtes de Blaye appellations. Wines from Blaye are much more varied than those from Bourg, as the vineyards are more spread out and the soil types less homogeneous. Blaye's wine are made for immediate consumption.

CHATEAUX IN BOURG AND BLAYE

Château Falfas
33710 Bayon
Tel: 05 57 64 80 41 *(B2)*

Château La Grolet
33710 St-Ciers-de-Canesse
Tel: 05 57 42 11 95 *(B2)*

Château Haut-Bertinerie
33620 Cubnezais
Tel: 05 57 68 70 74 *(B5)*

Château Haut-Macô
33710 Tauriac
Tel: 05 57 68 81 26 *(B3)*

Château Haut-Mondésir/ Mondésir-Gazin
le Sablon, 33390 Plassac
Tel: 05 57 42 29 80 *(C1)*

Château les Jonqueyres
Courgeau No 7
33390 St-Paul-de-Blaye
Tel: 05 57 42 34 88 *(D2)*

Château Nodoz
33710 Tauriac
Tel: 05 57 68 41 03 *(B3)*

Château la Raz-Caman
33390 Anglade
Tel: 05 57 64 41 82 *(E1)*

Château Roland la Garde
La Garde
33390 St-Seurin-de-Cursac
Tel: 05 57 42 32 29 *(D1)*

PRICES: moderate to expensive

Fronsac and Canon-Fronsac

F ronsac combines some of Bordeaux's most memorable and unusually hilly landscapes with some of its most underrated wines. Fronsac was renowned for its forceful reds until the eighteenth century when it was eclipsed by near-neighbours Pomerol and St-Emilion.

Named after a fort

Fronsac is named after a (now dismantled) fort built in 769 for Charlemagne (c.742–814AD). Built on the 75m (246-foot) summit or *tertre* of Fronsac, this fort overlooked the point where the river Isle meets the larger Dordogne directly west of the fortified market town (or *bastide*) and tourist hub of Libourne.

The town of Fronsac does have an old port, now disused, from which wine was shipped in barrel until the mid-nineteenth century. Local wine merchants still use the warehouses there, and Fronsac town has many seventeenth-century houses.

Right Bank value

Fronsac and Canon-Fronsac are now being recognised as offering some of the best-value wines on Bordeaux's Right Bank. They are weighty, lively, reds, although they can take several years in bottle to soften. The Fronsac hills offer such varied exposure to the sun that clever winemakers can stagger the harvest, building up a variety of flavours and textures from which to make a single wine.

Enter the labyrinth

The Fronsac region is labyrinthine, but small, with no vineyard further than 13km (8 miles) from Libourne. Use the two main roads that traverse the region to get your bearings, then take minor roads off to explore the châteaux, which are mercifully well signposted.

The two main roads are: the D670 Libourne-St-André-de-Cubzac road (*see* route one on map, right) and the D10E/246 Fronsac-Villegouge road (*see* route two on map, right).

Travelling around

Route one: approximately 25km (15 miles) in length, this itinerary goes from Libourne to Fronsac, St-Michel-de-Fronsac, La Rivière, St-Germain-de-la-Rivière, and finishes in Cadillac-en-Fronsadais.

Route two: roughly 10km (6 miles) in length, this goes from Fronsac to Saillans via the *lieu-dit* of Vincent.

LOCAL INFORMATION

Syndicat d'Initiative Maison du Pays Fronsadais
1 Barrail de Tourenne
33240 St Germain-de-la-Rivière
Tel: 05 57 84 86 86
As well as providing free maps, the tourist office also sells wine from the Fronsadais vineyards. Follow signs for "Maison du Pays".

Maison des Vins
33126 Fronsac
Tel: 05 57 51 80 51
Wine shop run by the Canon-Fronsac and Fronsac growers. Can arrange winery visits.

Route one: Biodynamics and historic estates

From Libourne, take the D670, direction St-André-de-Cubzac, crossing over the river Isle towards the centre of Fronsac. As you approach Fronsac at Vierge, the road bends sharply to the right and there is a road to the left, running along the Dordogne. Take this to reach Fronsac's port and the offices of Michel Ponty (A2, 33145 St-Michel de Fronsac, tel: 05 57 51 29 57), source of an outstanding 100 per cent Merlot called Grand-Renouil. He also, unusually, makes fine white, too. Or, staying on the D670, on the left-hand side is the Biodynamic Château La Grave (A2, tel: 05 57 51 31 11), made by Paul Barre, whose other Biodynamic vineyard is La Fleur Cailleau.

Go through Fronsac. Pass through La Dauphine, and when you reach La Marche, turn right. After a few hundred metres on your right is the pretty nineteenth-century Château Junayme, best seen from its garden (tel: 05 57 51 16 13), and another hundred metres on the left is the friendly Noël family's consistent Château Barrabaque (A2, visits are by appointment; tel: 05 57 51 31 79, châteaubarrabaque @yahoo.fr).

Fronsac: route one
A pleasant half-day trip

Fronsac: route two
Half a day or more depending on the visits you fix up

0   1 Km
0   1 mile

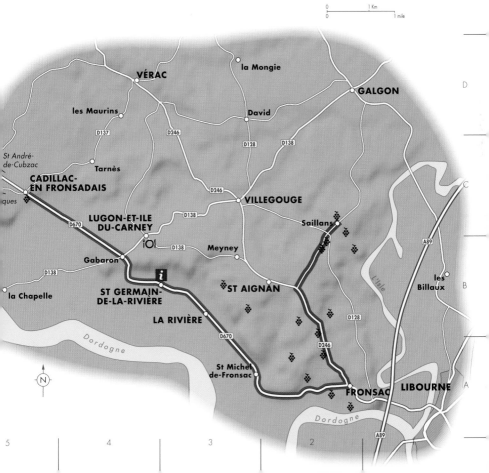

CHATEAUX IN FRONSAC AND CANON-FRONSAC

Château Branda
33240 Cadillac-en-
Fronsadais
Tel: 05 57 94 09 37 *(D5)*

Château de la Rivière
33126 La Rivière
Tel: 05 57 55 56 56 *(B3)*

Chateau Mazeris
33126 St-Michel-de-Fronsac
Tel: 05 57 24 98 25 *(B2)*

PRICES: moderate

Back on the D670, go through Naudin, the commune of St-Michel-de-Fronsac and then La Rivière. From the commune of Fronsac to the commune of La Rivière is less than 5km (3 miles). A small fork to the right just before the first of the commune's main buildings leads to the Davau family's tiny Château La Rousselle, producing concentrated reds (*B3*, 33126 St Germain-la-Rivière, tel: 05 57 24 96 73). The second right turn after you leave La Rivière leads to the thirteenth-century Château de la Rivière (*see left*). Look for signs to its "*caves*". These are dug into the soft limestone behind the château. Free daily visits.

Back on the D670 and into Cadillac-en-Fronsadais, is Château Branda (*see left*), built from 1360 onwards for Edward III, the English king who started the Hundred Years' War with France in 1337. There are modern art exhibitions, a medieval sensory "Garden of Delights", concerts and a wine exhibition, plus tasting and a shop. Open daily from Easter to November 1, and at weekends and bank holidays during the rest of the year; there is a charge.

Route two: dynamism and windmills

In Fronsac, take the right hand turn off the D670 onto the D246, direction Villegouge. The road climbs and after 1km (0.6 miles), on the left is the long driveway of Château du Gaby (*A2*, tel: 05 57 51 24 97), now owned by the Khayat family, related through marriage to the Weston family, owners of Fortnum & Mason in London. At the next left hand turn Château

BELOW *Fronsac's tranquil riverbanks afford fine views to Libourne across the rivers Isle and Dordogne.*

Moulin-Pey-Labrie (*B2*, tel: 05 57 51 14 37) is signposted, where the owners, the Hubau family, will let you taste their wines in their old windmill. Carry on along the D246 for 200m for a left-hand turn at a five-way crossing for the elegant wines and building of Château Mazeris (*see left*). A right hand turn at this crossroads takes you to the more value-oriented wines of Château Coustolle (*B2*, tel: 05 57 51 31 25).

Final stop is the commune of Saillans, which is reached by staying on the D246 as far as Vincent, and turning right onto the D246E4. Saillans is Fronsac's most dynamic commune. Château La Vieille Cure (*C2*, tel: 05 57 84 32 05) is first to appear on your right, with Château Moulin Haut-Laroque (*C2*, tel: 05 57 84 32 07), and then Château Villars (*C2*, tel: 05 57 84 32 17) almost immediately on the left. All produce consistently smooth, aromatic reds. Slightly further on, Château Fontenil (*C2*, tel: 05 57 51 23 05) is signposted on the left, owned by Michel Rolland. Château Dalem (*C2*, tel: 05 57 84 34 18) is almost opposite, and has a fabulous view over the Isle river and the Libournais

By foot and by water
The tourist office in St Germain-la-Rivière (*see* p.104) provides free maps for ramblers (a *randonée pédestre* is a walk or a ramble). Cross the low-lying farmland to find picnic benches near the Dordogne – beware mosquitoes. Between June and November, around full and new moon, the smooth on the Dordogne, the *mascaret*, is surfed by locals. Bring your own surfing gear.

Fronsac and Canon-Fronsac wine facts
Fronsac and Canon-Fronsac are collectively called the "Fronsadais". Canon-Fronsac wines come from vineyards directly overlooking the Dordogne on the region's purest limestone in the two communes of Fronsac and the nighbouring St-Michel-de-Fronsac. However, although some of the châteaux with the word "Canon" in their name have potentially fantastically well-sited vines, too many have lived too long on their reputations, so beware. Canon-Fronsacs are said to be superior to Fronsacs from the sandier limestone of the hinterland. This begins in La Rivière and St-Michel-de-Fronsac, continuing into hills around Saillans, St-Aignan, and Galgon. Around six million bottles of red wine are produced annually from 1,000ha of vines. A typical blend is Merlot, with up to twenty-five per cent Cabernet Franc, but only late-ripening Cabernet Sauvignon. The latter can struggle to ripen fully here every year; lower yields help.

WHERE TO EAT

For where to stay, *see* Libourne (p.112).

Le Bord d'Eau
33126 Fronsac
Tel: 05 57 51 99 91
Just off the D670
Libourne-Fronsac road.
Great view overlooking the Dordogne, with cuisine to match. Closed in September and November, and on Mondays and Wednesdays.

Auberge de la Vieille Chapelle
33240 Lugon et Ile du Carney
Tel: 05 57 84 48 65
Rich cuisine in an airy, twelfth-century chapel with a terrace overlooking the Dordogne. Closed on Tuesdays.

Libourne, Pomerol, and Lalande-de-Pomerol

Pomerol is Bordeaux's tiniest, but most exclusive red wine district. Made up of several hamlets, the centre is Trochau for churchgoers and the area between Catusseau, Maillet, and Pignon for wine-lovers. While there are a few grand châteaux here, like Châteaux Beauregard and de Sales, generally country houses and converted barns are the order of the day.

Post-war palate pleaser

Pomerol really only came to fame after World War II, when its lush, utterly approachable, Merlot-dominated red wines revived jaded Dutch, Belgian, and British palates in a period of austerity. The trailblazer was Pétrus, with its curiously nondescript winery and its house with ugly green shutters. This is now being challenged by micro-domaines like Château le Pin. This lies next to the Belgian Thienpont family's Vieux-Château-Certan, and is also Thienpont-owned. Le Pin has become such a cult wine, and is made in such small quantities, that a case can sell at auction for the price of a luxury sports car.

Feet of clay

The secret of Pomerol is the richness of the clay and the stones in the topsoil, perfect for the Merlot grape to show off its juniper-and-truffle scent. Pomerol's vines lie on a 35m (115-foot) high plateau, which stretches a short drive from Libourne's suburbs. The plateau is shaped like a female breast, with Pétrus, Vieux-Château-Certan, Certan-de-May, and Hosanna (formerly Certan-Giraud) sharing most of the nipple, with the exotic Château le Gay and Château Lafleur on the surrounds.

The clay-gravel mix becomes less favourable north of the Barbanne stream where the Lalande-de-Pomerol appellation begins. Rivalries between this region's two communes, Néac and Lalande, are surprisingly intense. Some (older) inhabitants make a point of never crossing the N89 road which divides the two. In view of the speed of the traffic, they're probably wise.

Roll out the barrel

Tucked away in a brick shed just off the N89 is Darnajou's cooperage, Bordeaux's finest barrel-

BELOW *The most celebrated Pomerol estate, Pétrus, is a nondescript building looking more like a private house. The keys represent those held by St Peter at the gates of heaven.*

maker. You'll know it by the vanilla-scented smoke of burning oak as the staves are bent into place.

Getting there

By train, Libourne is three hours from Paris on the TGV, or just twenty minutes from Gare St-Jean in Bordeaux. Or, by car, take the RN89 from Bordeaux, or the D936 from Bergerac. Parking a car in Libourne's narrow back-streets can be tricky, and especially on market days; try the underground car park on Place Abel Surchamp. The local traffic wardens are super-efficient. Short-stay tickets can be bought from street ticket machines.

Pomerol and Lalande-de-Pomerol

Fix up some visits to make a daytrip out of this inspiring area

Travelling around

About 19km (12 miles) in length, we head northeast from Libourne on the D910, over the Barbanne stream to Les Annereaux, turning right for Lalande-de-Pomerol, and then zigzaging on to Néac. We travel back across the Barbanne into Pomerol country, before going via the

WHERE TO EAT

Restaurant Le Merlot
86 rue Catusseau
33500 Pomerol
Tel: 05 57 74 11 20
Named after Pomerol's
pre-eminent grape.
Good place to spot –
and buttonhole – local
winemakers.

Chez Servais
14 place Decazes
33500 Libourne
Tel: 05 57 51 83 97
Varied menu in which
fish dishes are the most
consistent. In the heart
of the fortified town.
Closed Sunday evenings,
Mondays, and August
12–25.

Le Chai
20 place Decazes
33500 Libourne
Tel: 05 57 51 13 59
Generous wine list
complements "terroir" menu
of local specialities such as
rib steak with mushrooms.

Le Grill de l'Etrier
21 place Decazes
33500 Libourne
Tel: 05 57 51 26 99
Plush interior, with cooking
to match.

Brasserie Decazes
22 place Decazes
33500 Libourne
Tel: 05 57 25 18 70
Attracts a younger crowd
than some of its neighbours
on the place Decazes.

hamlets of Catusseau, Trochau (and the church), and Clocquet back to Libourne.

Leaving Libourne

From the centre of Libourne take the main D910 Libourne-Angoulême road. You can pick this up when approaching Libourne from Fronsac on the D670 St-André-de-Cubzac road. Cross the stone bridge, continue up rue de Président Wilson to the café-filled place Jean Moulin, and turn hard left at the big roundabout onto avenue Maréchal Foch (the D910).

After just over 2km (1 mile) the landscape changes from urban to more rural, and Château Mazeyres (see "châteaux to visit") is signposted on the right-hand side. This nineteenth-century château appears on one's left from the Paris-Libourne train. The scattered vineyards – which consist of three main plots on wildly different soil types – are skilfully blended into bright, fruit-laden reds for relatively earlyish drinking.

Lalande-de-Pomerol

From Château Mazeyres the D910 becomes known as the Avenue Georges Pompidou. Continue on it, passing Château de Sales (tel: 05 57 51 04 92) on the right, then crossing the Barbanne stream. Now you are in the Lalande-de-Pomerol appellation. Around 4km (2.5 miles) from Château Mazeyres you reach Les Annereaux. Here, you should turn right towards

RIGHT *Plane trees are a common feature of French provincial towns, offering shade in summer but ugly stumps after winter pruning.*

the commune of Lalande-de-Pomerol, crossing over the Bordeaux-Paris railway line.

Reaching the plateau

From the commune of Lalande-de-Pomerol travel 1.6km (1 mile) along the D245 to Château Grand-Ormeau (*see* right). This lies on the edge of the main Libourne-Périgueux N89 road. The château produces consistently well-made, Merlot-dominated (seventy per cent) reds, showing the silkiness Lalande-de-Pomerol's sandy-gravel soils can induce. From Château Grand-Ormeau turn right, and after just over 1km (half a mile) you reach Marchesseau. Turn left here onto the D121 to Néac, via the hamlet of Chevrol. This winding road overlooks the best part of Pomerol, the Plateau de Certan, from behind, as the land falls down to the Barbanne stream.

Across the Barbanne

Leaving Néac, stay on the D121 by bearing right to drop down and across the Barbanne. The land rises and you reach a crossroads. If you turn left here or go straight on you encounter, in what seems a blink of an eye, vineyards belonging to Pomerol's greatest and most famous names, such as Pétrus, Lafleur-Pétrus, La Fleur, and Le Gay.

But if you turn right at the first crossroads and immediately right again you arrive at the unprentious Château Gazin (*see* right). This château boasts beautifully restored cellars and outbuildings across gravelled courtyards, complete with a clocktower. Its underrated red wines are sold under the Gazin and Hospitalet de Gazin labels.

Approachable aristocracy

Turn left out of Château Gazin, then right at the first crossroads. On your left are the most gravelly vineyards of St-Emilion, such as Château Cheval Blanc. On your right are first Château L'Evangile, then Vieux-Château-Certan (*see* right). This is the least pretentious of Pomerol's aristocrats, bravely and successfully utilising Cabernet Franc to bolster its headier, but less-structured, Merlot. The oldest vines in the vineyards date from 1932.

Turn right out of Vieux-Château-Certan to reach the hamlet of Catusseau, which is less than 3km

CHATEAUX IN LIBOURNE, POMEROL, AND LALANDE

The following wineries welcome visitors, but by prior appointment only.

Château Gazin
33330 Pomerol
Tel: 05 57 51 07 05 *(B1)*
www.château-gazin.com
contact@gazin.com

Château Gombaude-Guillot
4 chemin des Grand Vignes
33500 Pomerol
Tel: 05 57 51 17 40 *(B2)*
château.gombaude-guillot@wanadoo.fr

Château Grand-Ormeau
33500 Lalande-de-Pomerol
Tel: 05 57 25 30 20 *(D2)*
grand-ormeau@wanadoo.fr

Château Mazeyres
54–56 avenue Georges Pompidou
33350 Libourne
Tel: 05 57 51 00 48 *(C4)*
mazeyres@wanadoo.fr

Vieux-Château-Certan
Catusseau
33330 Pomerol
Tel: 05 57 51 17 33 *(B2)*
info@vieuxchâteaucertan.com

PRICES: expensive

BED AND BREAKFAST:
M. and Mme. Ferranti
19 chemin des Ormeaux
33500 Pomerol
Tel: 05 57 25 99 67
Mobile: 06 66 87 81 97
ferranti.bf@wanadoo.fr
Quiet private house with
one double room.

Château Belles-Graves
33550 Néac
Tel: 05 57 51 09 61
www.belles-graves-com
x.piton@belles.graves.com
An eighteenth-century
château named after the
"beautiful gravel" in its
vineyard.

Château de Viaud
33500 Lalande
Tel: 05 56 91 80 80
Upmarket bed and
breakfast in sought-after
wine château.

**HOTELS: La Tour du
Vieux Port**
23 quai Souchet
33500 Libourne
Tel: 05 57 25 75 56
Comfortable hotel with
reliable restaurant open
to non-residents, located
in the heart of Libourne's
fortified waterfront.

Hôtel Decazes
22 place Decazes
33500 Libourne
Tel: 05 57 25 19 01
Modern but not soulless.
It was formerly called
the Hôtel Le Petit Duc.

Hôtel de la Gare
43 rue Chanzy
33500 Libourne
Tel: 05 57 51 06 86
No-frills hotel, plus
restaurant, for the
rail-weary.

(2 miles) from Néac. Giving way to the two roads on your right, but keeping Catusseau hamlet on your immediate left, take the D121 until you reach a crossroads around 300m later. You will have passed the nondescript Le Pin (yes, there really is a pine tree – or two, *see* p.25) up a short track on the right. At this crossroads turn right to Trochau which has the church spire as its landmark; indeed it's the only landmark in this part of Bordeaux.

Organics, and back to Libourne

On the way, Château Trotanoy will be on your left, while at Trochau you will see Château Gombaude-Guillot (*see* p.111) on the left when you come to a T-junction. Claire Laval has Pomerol's sole organic vineyard at Gombaude-Guillot. Her aromatic reds are reliant on notable proportions of Cabernet Franc, combined with the inevitable Merlot.

From Château Gombaude-Guillot turn left, and then right when you come to a crossroads after less than 200m. At the end of this road, at Clocquet, turn left on to the N89 for the 3.5km (2-mile) drive to the roundabout back at place Jean Moulin in Libourne.

Activities

The Libourne market is one of Bordeaux's best. Producers of paté, foie gras, vegetables, cheese, fruit (dried and fresh), flowers, pottery, crafts, and clothes come from all over southwest France to be here. The market takes place on Sunday, Tuesday, and Friday mornings, in the place Abel Surchamp, a large square surrounded by shops, private houses and the town's fifteenth-century Hôtel de Ville.

Quai du Priourat

The quayside in Libourne is home to some of Bordeaux's most powerful merchants: Janoueix, Horeau-Beylot, and most importantly Ets J-P. Moueix, which runs Pétrus and other star domaines in Pomerol and St-Emilion. Their warehouses run back from the quai du Priourat. Turn immediately right after crossing the stone bridge on the N89 when coming from Bordeaux. As you come over the bridge, you will see the silver-tiled Tour du Grand Port ("tower of the great harbour"). It formed part of the town's defences when the English controlled this part of Bordeaux and faced the French across the river Isle – indeed Libourne was founded by an Englishman called Leyburn in the thirteenth century.

Before that the area was a protectorate of the Knights of St John of the Cross (the Knights Templar) who established

a commandery here, not far from Domaine de l'Eglise (tel: 05 56 00 00 70). Stone crosses still to be seen in the vineyards guided pilgrims on their way to Santiago de Compostela in northern Spain.

The religious importance of this part of Bordeaux is remembered today in the names of many wines and wine estates. Numerous vineyards feature the name "La Croix" (the cross). L'Hospitalet de Gazin, second wine of Château Gazin (see p.111) refers to the "Hospitallers" or Knights of St John. Domaine de l'Eglise, Clos de l'Eglise and Clos de la Vieille l'Eglise are all vineyards carved out of former church land. Château Le Bon Pasteur means "the good shepherd" or "pastor".

Libourne, Pomerol, and Lalande de Pomerol wine facts

Pomerol covers less than 800ha of vines divided between around 200 growers. They produce around three million bottles of red wine annually. Lalande de Pomerol covers around 1,100ha of vines divided between 220 growers. Together they produce around six million bottles of red wine annually.

A typical blend for either region is sixty to eighty per cent Merlot, twenty to thirty-five per cent Cabernet Franc, with the rest either Malbec or Cabernet Sauvignon.

ABOVE *Libourne's main square, place Abel Surchamp, is home to a market held three times a week, and a good tourist office (see below).*

LOCAL INFORMATION
· ·

Office de Tourisme
place Abel Surchamp
33500 Libourne
Tel: 05 57 51 15 04
officedetourisme@
wanadoo.fr
With no Maison du Vin in Pomerol, try the tourist office in Libourne's main square instead for maps and guides. Remember that Libourne lies within the St-Emilion appellation, so ask here for information on that region, too.

St-Emilion

St-Emilion drips with history, wine, tourists; and if what they say is true, the mattresses of the local wine-growers drip with gold, too. This is one of the prettiest and most visited of French wine towns. It was declared a UNESCO World Heritage site in 1999. It is set in gentle, vine-clad hills overlooking the Dordogne valley. The town became a place of pilgrimage after the hermit Emilian settled here over 1,000 years ago. Close to his grotto is St-Emilion's ninth-century monolithic church, hewn from the soft, golden limestone upon which the town sits, and which was used to build the town.

Tourist heaven

The square in front of the church, place de l'Eglise Monolithe, and the square above, the place du Clocher underneath the church's more modern belltower, are surrounded by eateries and shops. Tourists outnumber the locals. The town of St-Emilion is tiny – fewer than 4,000 people live here – but has a very vibrant feel, despite its years of history. Some of the region's best wines are made in tiny quantities by younger wine-growers, following the 1990s fashion for "garage" wines that gave St-Emilion new impetus, and a real Burgundian feel. Many of the winery owners here pride themselves on working their vines, saying that their peers on the Left Bank are nothing but lazy, office-bound paper-pushers.

BELOW *This five-metre high menhir in St-Sulpice-de-Faleyrens is located at Port de Pierrefitte.*

Price to pay

Don't expect to understand St-Emilion in half a morning, such is its vastness and intricacy, and don't expect your visit to be cheap either. Save money by staying in Libourne or Castillon and making the short journey in. It will leave you more money to spend on the wines. Avoid buying from local wine shops, as most offer imperfect storage. But you will only begin to get a discount buying direct from growers if you buy several cases, and you pay cash. After all, those mattresses must be kept full.

Rich variety

The vineyards surrounding the limestone plateau either side of St-Emilion stretch for miles. The limestone gives the local reds their bright, vibrant character. Westwards, towards Libourne, the soil is gravelly, and the wines from Château Figeac (www.château-figeac.com) and Château Cheval Blanc (tel: 05 57 55 55 55) are more obviously rich and plummy, and more like those of Pomerol next door. The soils are gradually sandier as one approaches the Dordogne and the D670, and the wines become lighter. They are heaviest on the clay soils to the north of

Map labels:

5   4   3   2   1

Petit Palais

N89

les Artigues de Lussac

Malydure

D22   D17   D122   D21   A

Lavié

Font Muret

Lussac   B

Roques   Côtes de Francs

Bertineau   D244

Néac

D122   Montagne   Puisseguin

D244   St-Georges

Borbonne   D130   C

Pomerol   le Cros

D243   Parsac

LIBOURNE   St-Christophe-de-Bardes

Côtes de Castillon

D670   ST-EMILION   D243   D

D245

N89   St Hippolyte

D19   St-Étienne-de-Lisse

St-Laurent-des-Combes   N

St-Sulpice-de-Faleyrens   E

D670

0   1   2 Km
0   1   2 miles

Vignonet   the   St-Emilion

town   Allow a couple of days
to really enjoy St-Emilion
and its many wine highlights

D936   where

the plateau   F

Dordogne   descends to the

Branne   Barbanne stream. Position

is thus key to understanding the style of a château's wine.

Solid as a rock

Around the town and towards neighbouring villages like St-Christophe-des-Bardes and St-Laurent-des-Combes, limestone dominates. Vineyards closest to the town, like Ausone (tel: 05 57 24 70 26) whose stone pillars you pass on the left on the way from the D670, and Pavie (vignobles.perse@wanadoo.fr) which is further away and to the right, enjoy some of the best vineyard sites – natural sun traps – in France.

LOCAL INFORMATION

Office de Tourisme de St-Emilion
place des Créneaux
33330 St-Emilion
Tel: 05 57 55 28 28
www.st-emilion-tourisme.com
st-emilion.tourisme@wanadoo.fr

Syndicat Viticole de St-Emilion
rue Guadet
33330 St-Emilion
Tel: 05 57 55 50 50
www.vins-st-emilion.com
info@vins-st-emilion.com
St-Emilion's wine-growers' union is the oldest of its type in France.

BELOW *St-Emilion's most expensive wines come from the slopes that surround the town, while the best vineyards on the Dordogne plain provide relative value.*

Getting there

By car St-Emilion is less than 7km (5 miles) from Libourne on the D670. Trains from Libourne, destination Sarlat, take less than fifteen minutes.

Travelling around (*see* p.115)

Our route is 113 km (70 miles) in length. We start in Libourne and go to nearby Les Bigaroux, before heading off in earnest to Vignonet, St-Emilion town, east towards St-Christophe-des-Bardes returning to St-Emilion town to head north to Montagne St-Emilion, then Lussac St-Emilion, Les-Artigues-de-Lussac, Puisseguin St-Emilion, Parsac, through St-Christophe-des-Bardes, before reaching St-Laurent-des-Combes, and finally back to St-Emilion or on to Libourne.

Libourne to St-Emilion

Leave Libourne on the D670 Bergerac road. Just before a huge Carrefour supermarket, turn right onto Boulevard de Garderose. After 300m (980 feet) turn left onto Chemin Gueyrosse, at the end of which is Château Gueyrosse (*see* right). Yves Delol ferments handpicked grapes in small stone vats with natural yeasts. The wines are subtle, and very successful.

Back on the D670 head towards St-Emilion for less than 8km (5 miles) to Les Bigaroux. Turn right onto the D122, direction Branne. On the right-hand side after less than 1.6km (1 mile) is Château Bertinat-Lartigue (*see* right). Here Richard and Danielle Dubois produce smooth St-Emilion and, from vines across the appellation border, they make Côtes de Castillon reds in small stone vats.

Around Vignonet

Stay on the D122 signed to the Branne bridge over the Dordogne, but turn left just before the bridge to Vignonet on the D936. Turn left at Vignonet church before the roundabout. Go straight ahead to the stone cross. This is on the edge of Château Haut-Brisson's vineyard. At the cross turn left and then immediately right, and less than 100m (330 feet) from the cross is Château Haut-Brisson itself (see right). Resisting the modern temptation on the St-Emilion plain to make extracted, oaky wines to win blind-tasting competitions, Château Haut-Brisson favours something lighter – and more pleasurable to drink.

Head back towards St-Emilion on what becomes the D122E6, crossing over the D670. Turn left just before the railway line for Château Canon la Gaffelière (see right). This well-run estate with German owners is reverting to fermentation in wooden vats, Burgundy-style, to produce soft reds.

In St-Emilion

Continue up to St-Emilion, going right through the town. The tourist office here is very useful (see left). Ask here about bike hire, and for guided tours of St-Emilion's many historic monuments, such as the monolithic church and its catacombs. Ask also about where to buy, and see made, the local macaroon biscuits, first made from almonds, sugar, and egg-whites by Ursuline nuns in the seventeenth century. Guided tours in French and English are offered to local vineyards, with tastings, in May, June, and September. A fee is payable for these.

Going underground

At the top of St-Emilion's main road, before you get to the roundabout, is rue Guadet. Château Guadet-St-Julien is on the right hand side at number 4 and there is a small public car park nearby (see right). The Lignac family's underground cellars, which you can visit, were dug from 1791. The château makes handpicked, punchy reds.

Next door to Guadet-St-Julien is a wine merchant office and shop owned by Jean-Luc Thunevin, now one of Bordeaux's leading figures because of his creation of the *garagiste* micro-wine, Château de Valandraud which, like le Pin in Pomerol, sells for astronomical prices.

Roundabout St-Emilion

From the small St-Emilion roundabout take the right turn to St-Christophe-des-Bardes on the D17E. Château Soutard appears on your left after less than 1.6 km (1 mile) (see right). The talkative François des Ligneris of Château Soutard worked for the Red Cross in Vietnam before taking over here. His red wines are laden with soft fruit and smooth tannins.

CHATEAUX IN ST-EMILION

Château Balestard-La Tonnelle
33330 St-Emilion
Tel: 05 57 74 62 06 *(D3)*

Château Bellisle-Mondotte
33330 St-Laurent-des-Combes
Tel: 05 57 24 73 23 *(D3)*

Château Bertinat-Lartigue
33330 St-Sulpice-de-Faleyrens
Tel: 05 57 24 72 75 *(E3)*

Château Calon St-Georges
33330 St-Georges-St-Emilion
Tel: 05 57 51 64 88 *(C3)*

Château Canon la Gaffelière
33330 St-Emilion
Tel: 05 57 24 71 33 *(D3)*

Château La Croix-Beauséjour
33330 Montagne-St-Emilion
Tel: 05 57 74 69 62 *(B2)*

Château Fonroque
33330 St-Emilion
Tel: 05 57 51 78 96 *(C3)*

Château Guadet-St-Julien
4 Rue Guadet
33330 St-Emilion
Tel: 05 57 74 40 04 *(D3)*

Château Gueyrosse
33330 Libourne
Tel: 05 57 51 02 63 *(D5)*

Château Haut-Brisson
33330 Vignonet
Tel: 05 57 84 69 57 *(E3)*

Château Soutard
33330 St-Emilion
Tel: 05 57 24 72 23 *(D3)*

Château Trocard
33330 Les Artigues de Lussac
Tel: 05 57 55 57 98 *(A2)*

Château Beauséjour/Langlais
33570 Puisseguin St-Emilion
Tel: 05 57 74 52 61 *(C1)*

PRICES: expensive

WHERE TO EAT

Bistro le Clocher
3 place du Clocher
33330 St-Emilion
Tel: 05 57 74 43 04
Book ahead to get a seat
outside on the square
underneath the church.

Envers du Décor
11 rue du Clocher (just
off place des Creneaux)
33330 St-Emilion
Tel: 05 57 74 48 31
There's good food and
excellent wines by the
glass here – if you can
get served. Closed
Saturdays and Sundays.

L'Huitrier Pie
11 rue Porte Bouqueyre
33330 St-Emilion
Tel: 05 57 24 69 71
huitrierpie@free.fr
Oyster restaurant with
children's menu. Wash
your hands before you
hit the wine cellars.
Closed Wednesdays
and in February.

Logis de la Cadène
3 place du Marché au Bois
33330 St-Emilion
Tel: 05 57 24 71 40
St-Emilion staple tucked
away in an eighteenth-
century house in the high
part of the town. Closed
Sunday evenings and
Mondays.

Pizzeria de la Tour
19 rue de la Grande
Fontaine
33330 St-Emilion
Tel: 05 57 24 68 91
Family/child-friendly
pizzeria with good
pizzas plus homemade
foie gras. Closed on
Wednesdays.

Almost opposite Château Soutard is Château Balestard-la-Tonnelle (*see* p.117). The Capdemourlin family is one of St-Emilion's most historic and respected. They make classic wines from St-Emilion's limestone plateau. The vineyard tower here is seventeenth-century.

Then head back to rejoin our route at the St-Emilion roundabout, heading towards Montagne St-Emilion on the D122. Château Fonroque is signposted on the left after less than 2.25km (1.4 miles; *see* p.117). The earnest Alain Moueix of Fonroque is one of the most able vineyard managers in Bordeaux. At this

estate Merlot (eighty-eight per cent) and Cabernet Franc (twelve per cent) combine effortlessly to produce increasingly dramatic wines.

Happy camping

As you cross over the Barbanne stream on the D122 St-Emilion-Montagne road, you pass signposts to the fun Domaine de la Barbanne campsite. With a heated pool, tennis court, mini-golf, and a launderette, there are also mobile homes for rent and a free shuttle to St-Emilion. Open from April 1 to mid-September (www.camping-saint-emilion.com).

Château Calon-St-Georges lies off the first left-hand turn over the Barbanne, down the third road on the right (*see* p.117). The Boidron family own vines in St-Georges, Montagne, and St-Emilion. They make crisp, medium-bodied reds which represent the area well.

From Château Calon St-Georges stay on the D122, following signs to Lussac. Château la Croix-Beauséjour is down the first left-hand fork as you leave Montagne (*see* p.117). Olivier Laporte's 7ha vineyard is planted with Merlot (seventy-five per cent) plus Cabernet Franc, Cabernet Sauvignon, and Malbec. Fairly priced, light, elegant wines.

Once in Lussac, take the D22 to Les-Artigues-de-Lussac. At the crossroads in the centre of town turn right onto the D121 to Petit Palais. Vignobles Trocard is almost immediately on the right (*see* p.117). Here Jean-Louis Trocard is a reliable producer of Pomerol, Lalande de Pomerol, and Lussac-St-Emilion. The winery also has a spacious tasting area.

Organic option

Stay on the D22, then take the D122 back to Lussac. In Lussac, turn left onto the D17 signed to Puisseguin. Château Beauséjour/Langlais is on your left as you reach Puisseguin (see p.117). The Dupuy family bought Château Beauséjour before the Revolution, and later added Château Langlais (not to be confused with Château L'Anglais). Both are organic, handpicked, and generously flavoured.

From Puisseguin, take the D130 to Parsac and St-Christophe-des-Bardes. Here you are getting back on the main St-Emilion plateau, northeast of the town.

From St-Christophe, turn left onto the D243, then right onto the D243E2, turning right at the crossroads for Château Bellisle-Mondotte (see p.117). The Escure family's ripe, well-made, well-priced wines show how worthwhile it is to explore St-Emilion's ancillary communes. Take the D245 to St-Emilion. Turn right at the T-junction to go back to St-Emilion, or right and right again for Libourne.

A good place to unwind, and to meet younger members of wine families is the BDL (Bois de l'Or) night club. Steer clear of the sangria, though (Libourne-Bergerac road, tel: 05 57 51 35 43).

St-Emilion wine facts

St-Emilion is one of the largest wine regions of its type in France, with around 5,000ha of vines. The eight villages in the St-Emilion jurisdiction are Libourne (see Pomerol p.108), Vignonet, St-Sulpice-de-Faleyrens, St-Laurent-des-Combes, St-Christophe-des-Bardes, St-Hippolyte, St-Etienne-de-Lisse, and St-Emilion. They produce around thirty million bottles of red wine annually, with almost as much again coming from the satellite villages of Lussac, Montagne, St-Georges, and Puisseguin across the Barbanne stream to the north.

LEFT *The north entrance to St-Emilion's collegiate church.*

LEFT *Vines and wheat around a pair of early nineteenth century windmills.*

Côtes de Castillon and Côtes de Francs

The hills due east of St-Emilion conceal two small vineyard regions gaining increasing renown, especially for succulent red wines: Côtes de Castillon and the smaller Côtes de Francs. The landscape is dotted with fortified look-out towers and impressive castles. These are testaments to this area's battleground history, first under the Franks (hence the name of the hamlet of Francs) at the end of the first millennium, and then as the English and French fought for control of Aquitaine in the fifteenth century, with the English finally losing at the Battle of Castillon in 1453.

The morning after the night before

The English are said to have lost the Battle of Castillon because they raided local wine cellars on the eve of battle and were still hungover when the French attacked early the following morning. A small, rather unkempt monument to the victory can be seen by following the small road along the river Dordogne from Castillon's stone bridge. The Castillon hills, or côtes, offer some superb vineyard sites, with good drainage and excellent exposure to the sun. The district of Francs to the north is Bordeaux's driest region, and the red wines here can be heady, and the whites occasionally exotic. Wine-growers here have over the last decade become an increasingly quality-minded bunch, and their best wines offer much better value for money than the majority of everyday St-Emilions.

BELOW *To reach the Battle of Castillon monument turn left before Castillon's stone bridge on the Dordogne's north bank and follow the road for about 1.5km (1 mile).*

Wine information

The Castillon tourist office (see right) can coordinate winery visits in both Côtes de Castillon and Côtes de Francs. It may also direct you to the local wine-growers' syndicate, the Syndicat Viticole des Côtes de Castillon.

Getting there

By car, the town of Castillon-la-Bataille is 45km (28 miles) east of Bordeaux. It takes less than an hour by road from Bordeaux, via Libourne and St-Emilion on the N89 then D670.

Trains from Gare St-Jean in Bordeaux take less than an hour to reach Castillon-la-Bataille.

By bus, take CITRAM Aquitaine's Ligne 302 to Libourne and change there onto Ligne 402 for Castillon-la-Bataille. The service runs Mondays to Fridays onlys, with three per day.

Travelling around

We have chosen three short routes for this hilly area, all leaving from the region's central town, Castillon-la-Bataille.

Route one: approximately 10km (6 miles) in length, we start off heading east from Castillon-la-Bataille, through the far eastern edges of Belvès-de-Castillon and Gardengan-et-Tourtirac, as far as Les-Salles-de-Castillon.

Route two: about 5km (3 miles) long, heading west from Castillon-la-Bataille to St-Magne-de-Castillon and slightly beyond.

Route three: roughly 13km (8 miles) long, we begin by heading north from Castillon-la-Bataille, through the western edge of Belvès-de-Castillon and Gardegan-et-Tourtirac, and the eastern edge of St-Philippe d'Aiguilhe, into the village of St-Cibard.

LOCAL INFORMATION

Office du Tourisme
place Marcel Paul
33350 Castillon-La-Bataille
Tel: 05 57 40 27 58
tourismecastillonlabataille@
wanadoo.fr

Syndicat Viticole des Côtes de Castillon
6 allées de la République
33350 Castillon-la-Bataille
Tel: 05 57 40 00 88
svcc@vins-bordeaux.fr

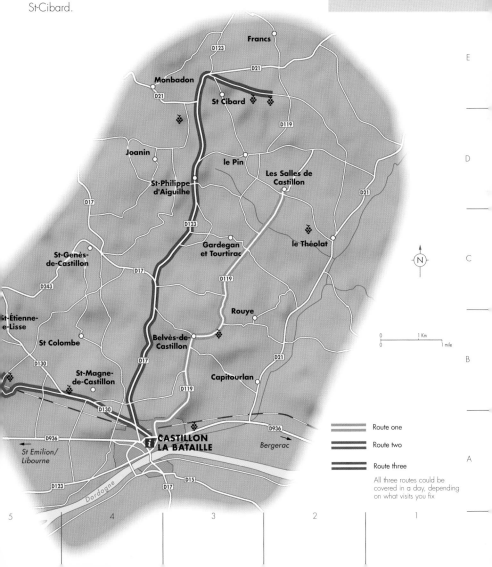

CHATEAUX IN COTES DE CASTILLON AND FRANCS

Château Brandeau
33350 Les Salles de Castillon
Tel: 05 57 40 65 48 *(C2)*

Château Fontbaude
34 rue de l'Eglise
33350 St-Magne-de-Castillon
Tel: 05 57 40 06 58 *(B4)*
château.fontbaude@
wanadoo.fr

Château Les Moulins de Coussillon
Godard
33570 Francs
Tel: 05 57 40 65 77 *(E4)*

Château Peyrou
33350 St-Magne-de-Castillon
Tel: 05 57 24 72 05 *(B5)*

Château Puygueraud
Lauriol, 33570 St-Cibard
Tel: 05 57 56 07 47 *(E3)*
ch.puygueraud@wanadoo.fr

Château Seigneur de Ganeau
141 rue Michel Montaigne
33350 Castillon-la-Bataille
Tel: 05 57 40 02 05 *(A3)*
Pierrick.Brachem@
wanadoo.fr

PRICES: Moderate to expensive

Route one: the artisan approach

From Castillon-la-Bataille, take the D936 towards Bergerac/Ste-Foy-la-Grande. Château Seigneur de Ganeau (see left) is on the left-hand side of the road. Pierreck Brachem of this estate is an enthusiastic, small-scale grower working from his house located on the outskirts of Castillon-la-Bataille.

After less than 3km (2 miles) from the town centre turn left onto the D21 towards Villefranche de Lonchat. Continue for approximately 4.5km (3 miles) and turn left when you see signs for Les Salles de Castillon. The first winery on the left is Château Brandeau (see left). This is the oldest certified organic vineyard in Côtes de Castillon, and organic beef is available too. English is spoken here.

Route two: old vines and value

From Castillon-la-Bataille take the D130, direction St-Emilion. Château Fontbaude (see left) appears on the right on the western edge of St-Magne-de-Castillon. The Sabaté-Zavan family produce value-for-money reds.

Leave the D130 by bearing left at the next fork. Cross the railway line and take the next right for Château Peyrou (see left). Made from weedkiller-free vines dating from 1956, Catherine Papon-Nouvel's wines show both ripeness and purity.

RIGHT *Traditionally Castillon wines were shipped in barrel on the Dordogne, hence the anchor.*

Route three: characters that age well

Take the D17 Coutras road from Castillon-la-Bataille and bear right on the fork to the D123 after nearly 5km (3 miles). Continue for another 6km (4 miles), passing signs for the friendly Lavau family's Château Terrasson (www.vignobles-lavau.com) on the left-hand side. The road is now the D21, which after 1.6km (1 mile) runs north of St-Cibard, which is in the Côtes de Francs.

To get to Château Les Charmes Godard, follow signs to the *lieu-dit* Lauriol. To get to Château Les Moulins de Coussillon follow signs to the *lieu-dit* Godard (*see* left). Bernadette and Joseph Arbo of this estate spend most of their time in their vines, so call ahead to taste a highly individual wine range, including the dry white Château Puyanché and the Merlot-dominated Moulins de Coussillon.

At Château Puygueraud the Thienpont family produce ageworthy reds and succulent dry whites from a fourteenth-century manor-house (*see* left).

Son-et-Lumière

A spectacular reconstruction of the 1453 Battle of Castillon takes place on Fridays and Saturdays from July 15 to August 15 each year. Eight-hundred volunteers, including 500 actors and more than fifty horsemen, take part in a two-hour-long show. The venue is Château Castegens: take the D119 to Belvès-de-Castillon which runs from the Castillon railway station. Book by telephone: 05 57 40 14 53.

Get on a horse

The owners of Château Blanzac run a pony club, Centre Equestre et Poney Club (Ecuries de Blanzac, 22 route de Coutras, 33350 St-Magne-de-Castillon; tel: riding, 05 57 40 28 52, or wine visits, 05 57 40 11 89). Situated just north of Castillon-la-Bataille on the D17 Coutras road. Or just follow the hoofprints.

Pedal power

There are cycle-hire shops in Castillon-la-Bataille and St-Magne-de-Castillon which also provide guidance on the best

WHERE TO STAY

(*See* also "where to eat")

HOTELS:
La Bonne Auberge
6 rue du 8 mai 1945
33350 Castillon-la-Bataille
Tel: 05 57 40 11 56

Les Voyageurs
allées de la République
(opposite the church)
33350 Castillon-la-Bataille
Tel: 05 57 40 10 51

BED AND BREAKFAST:
Francis Bonneaud
le Bourg
33350 Belvès-de-Castillon
Tel: 05 57 47 96 02
francis.bonneaud@wanadoo.fr
Part of a wine estate located 1km (half a mile) from the site of the Battle of Castillon. Be sure to book well in advance during summer.

CAMPSITE:
Camping La Pelouse
33350 Castillon-la-Bataille
Tel: 05 57 40 04 22
Located next to the Dordogne, overlooked by the town's stone bridge.

WHERE TO EAT

Castillon is not a
gastronomic heartland,
and most locals go to
St-Emilion and Libourne
when treating themselves.

Les Pyrénées
10 rue Michel Montaine
33350 Castillon-la-Bataille
Tel: 05 57 40 01 42

Pizzeria Le Mounan
20 bis rue des Frères Bureau
33350 Castillon-la-Bataille
Tel: 05 57 40 38 19
Pizzeria equipped with
wood-fired ovens.

Chez Clovis
D670 Lavagnac
33350 Ste-Terre
Tel: 05 57 47 16 03
Simple hotel-restaurant
west of Castillon,
offering good set menus
on Sundays.

Boulangerie Gava
D670 Lavagnac
tel: 05 57 47 16 18
Worth making a beeline to
this bakery which produces
superb baguettes and
cakes

BELOW *The limestone
of St-Emilion: good for
buildings, good for wine.*

local cycle routes. Casticycles (6 avenue John Talbot, 33350
Castillon- la-Bataille, tel: 05 57 40 36 40); or Gauthier Cycles
(13 avenue Europe, 33350 St-Magne-de-Castillon, tel: 05 57
40 12 27).

Water sports
The Canoeing-Rowing Club Castillonnais offers courses lasting
as little as two hours in either rowing boats (*bateaux d'aviron*)
or canoes (quai André Duranton, 33350 Castillon-la-Bataille,
tel: 05 57 40 23 68, www.rccastillon.com.)

Take a walk
At the tourist office in Castillon-la-Bataille (see p.121) you can
pay a nominal sum for a small map outlining one of eight local
routes for walkers and ramblers. The most popular is the 10km
(6-mile) route running from the Castillon-la-Bataille campsite
located on the quayside by the Dordogne up into the hills
of Belvès-de-Castillon to reach the site of the Battle of Castillon.

Côtes de Castillon wine facts
Côtes de Castillon has about 3,000ha of vines in nine
designated communes: Belvès-de-Castillon, Castillon-la-Bataille,
Gardegan-et-Tourtirac, Les Salles de Castillon, Monbadon,
St-Genès-de-Castillon, St-Magne-de-Castillon, St-Philippe
d'Aiguille, and Ste-Colombe.
    The area has around 350 wine-growers producing an
average of twenty million bottles of wine annually. Red wines
are labelled Côtes de Castillon, while dry whites are simply
labelled Bordeaux.

Côtes de Francs wine facts
Côtes de Francs has just under 550ha of vines in the three
communes of St-Cibard, Tayac and Francs, ninety-five per cent
of which is for red wine. Around three million bottles are
produced each year by fewer than thirty growers. Côtes de
Francs white wines can be either dry or
medium-dry.
    Most reds from these two regions
are composed of two thirds or more
Merlot, with Cabernets Franc and
Sauvignon making up the rest of the
blend. Sémillon and Sauvignon Blanc
are the mainstays of the whites.

Premières Côtes de Bordeaux, Cadillac, Loupiac, and Ste-Croix-du-Mont

T he vineyards surveying the Garonne from the hills to the east belong to the Premières Côtes region; and just as Bourg and Blaye suffer in comparison with the more highly regarded vineyards of the Médoc across the Gironde, so the Premières Côtes suffer in comparison with the wines of Pessac-Léognan and Barsac-Sauternes across the Garonne.

The English influence

Yet during the middle ages the Premières Côtes matched the Graves in establishing Bordeaux wine as a favourite of the English crown. The fourteenth-century fortified town walls and towers at Cadillac are a reminder of how the English and French fought for control of the Garonne. These days much of the northern Premières Côtes is covered by urban sprawl from Bordeaux. Most of the better vineyard sites there are built over now, but during the middle ages wine from communes like Carbon-Blanc, Ste-Eulalie, Yvrac, Lormont, Cénon, Floirac, and Bouliac was sought out by Bordeaux merchants to add structure to their blends. Now, merchants and tourists must begin their vinous searches further south: as a generalization the best reds come from between Latresne and Rions, while south of Béguey dry, medium-dry and sweet whites are prized.

It's a breeze

Wine has been made here since Roman times, and many villages have Roman remains. The region's hills are made of soft limestone, which have been burrowed out over centuries – there are caves, for example, at Ste-Croix-du-Mont. Ask at the Ste-Croix tourist office for information on visits to these.

The Premières Côtes were formed by the same glacial movements which brought the famous gravel to the Graves and Pessac-Léognan regions on the opposite bank of the Garonne. Although the slopes of the Premières Côtes vineyards have less gravel than Graves and Pessac-Léognan, their trump card is the height of the slopes. They allow the vineyards to catch both sun and wind. Stiff breezes from the northwest or northeast concentrate the flavours in the best grapes. This is especially true of the northern Premières Côtes. Further south around the more sheltered slopes of Loupiac, Cadillac, and Ste-Croix-du-

LOCAL INFORMATION

Office du Tourisme
place de la Libération
33410 Cadillac
Tel: 05 56 62 12 92

Office du Tourisme
5 place du Docteur
Abaut, 33550 Langoiran
Tel: 05 56 67 56 18

Syndicat d'Initiative
place du 8 mai 1945
33310 Lormont
Tel: 05 56 74 29 17

Maison du Pays de St-Macaire
8 rue du Canton
33490 St-Macaire
Tel: 05 56 63 32 14

Mont river mists form to encourage the noble rot fungus (*see* Barsac-Sauternes and Cérons, p.91) upon which great sweet white wines rely.

Perfect match

Soil types vary widely, so each grape variety must be matched perfectly to its part of the vineyard: Cabernet Sauvignon on the warm, sheltered part of the mid-slopes; Merlot on bright, limestone pebbles with clay underneath, and Cabernet Franc on clay lower down, nearer (but not too near) the Garonne.

Sémillon and Sauvignon Blanc prefer limestone and clay, so as not to overheat and lose their valuable aromas. Denis Dubourdieu of Château Reynon (*see* p.128) is one of the world's experts on the aromas of these two grapes in particular, and of white wine in general.

Getting there

By car from the north you could follow the route suggested below. From the south it's better to aim for Langon, and cross the Garonne there; or cross the Garonne via the bridges that link the towns of Cérons and Cadillac, and those of Portets and Langoiran.

Travelling around

Roughly 80km (50 miles) in length, we start by going southeast from Bordeaux and go along the Premières Côtes on the D10, through Latresne, then Cambes, off at le Tourne,

The slopes of the Garonne
A day will give a good insight into this interesting area

to Capian, rejoining the D10 at Beguey, then Cadillac, Ste-Croix-du-Mont, up to St-Maixant, and ending up in Verdelais.

LEFT *Go for the dry whites with oysters; semi-sweet whites will not be a success.*

Bordeaux to Cambes

From Bordeaux cross over the Garonne and head south on the D113 to Langon. Turn left at the first roundabout after Latresne for Château Le Parvis du Domaine Tapiau (*see* p.128). Olivier Reumaux's domaine dates from just before the Revolution. He grows organic grapes, uses traditional fermentation in stone vats for generous reds. Continue south on the D113, which becomes the D10 before Cambes. In the village of Cambes take the road on the right opposite l'Auberge André, and Château Puy Bardens is just 1km (half a mile) on the left (*see* p.128). Yves Lamiable's chunky red wines are perfect for Bordeaux's favourite dinner: rib-steak grilled over vine prunings.

Cambes to Beguey

From Cambes continue for just over 5.5km (3 miles) on the D10 to Le Tourne, then take a left to Capian on the D13. From Capian stay on the D13, direction Créon, and after 2km (1.2 miles) Château Plaisance appears on the left (*see* p.128). Patrick and Sabine Bayle produce apricot-flavoured Ste-Croix-du-Mont and bright reds based on Cabernet Sauvignon, Cabernet Franc, and Merlot, in which oak and fruit are seamlessly combined.

From Capian take the D13, direction Beguey. As the road descends to Beguey, Château Reynon's large stone gateway is on the right, before the cemetery. Denis Dubourdieu is one of the world's leading winemakers, and a professor at Bordeaux University. Château Reynon produces a huge range of wines from vines in the Premières Côtes, Cadillac and the Graves region across the Garonne. They include inspiring, aromatic whites and reliable reds.

WHERE TO EAT

LUXURY: La Cape
allée de la Morlette
33150 Cénon
Tel: 05 57 80 24 25
Modern decor to match modern-style cooking. Try pig's trotter pancakes (*galettes*). Closed August 1–23, Christmas holidays, weekends and public holidays.

MEDIUM-PRICED: La Maison du Fleuve
20 chemin Seguin
Port Neuf 33360
Camblanes-et-Meynac
Tel: 05 56 20 06 40
Riverside bistro with good non-Bordeaux wine list.

L'Entrée du Jardin
27 rue Pont
33410 Cadillac
Tel: 05 56 76 96 96
Popular choice with local wine-growers. The daily set menus offer good value.

Auberge du Marais
22 route de Latresne
33270 Bouliac
Tel: 05 56 20 52 17
Gascon-style cooking here is richer than the Gironde norm. Closed August 2–31, February 20 to March 6, Sunday evenings and Mondays.

AVERAGE-PRICED: Café de l'Esperance
derrière l'église
33270 Bouliac
Tel: 05 56 20 52 16
Good for grilled steaks; atmospheric and fairly priced.

CHATEAUX IN P. COTES, CADILLAC, LOUPIAC, STE-CROIX

Château du Juge
route de Branne
33410 Cadillac
Tel:05 56 62 17 77 *(B3)*
pierre.dupleich@wanadoo.fr

Château le Parvis de Domaine Tapiau
33360 Camblanes et Meynac
Tel: 05 56 20 15 62 *(D1)*
Leparvis@wanadoo.fr

Château de Plaisance
33550 Capian
Tel: 05 56 72 15 06 *(D3)*
contact@châteauplaisance.fr

Château Puy Bardens
33880 Cambes
Tel: 05 56 21 31 14 *(D2)*
château-puybardens@
wanadoo.fr

Château La Rame La Charmille
33410 Ste-Croix-du-Mont
Tel: 05 56 62 01 50 *(A4)*
dgm@wanadoo.fr

Château Reynon
21 route de Cardan
33410 Beguey
Tel: 05 56 62 96 51 *(C3)*
reynon@gofornet.com

Domaines Tich et Grava
Domaine du Tich
33490 Verdelais
Tel: 05 56 62 05 42 *(A4)*
fonteyreaud.vins
debordeaux@wanadoo.fr

PRICES: moderate to expensive

Beguey to Cadillac

From Beguey, take the D10 south to Cadillac. As you leave the south side of the town, and in front of the ramparts, turn right at the roundabout where many local châteaux are signposted left; turn left onto the route de Branne, and just as the landscape becomes more rural, Château du Juge is on the right (*see left*). Pierre Dupleich produces unusually buttery-tasting dry whites, concentrated sweet Cadillacs, and good range of reds at this rambling estate.

Around Ste-Croix-du-Mont

From Cadillac, take the D10 south to Ste-Croix-du-Mont, but ignore the first set of signs for Ste-Croix-du-Mont, its church and caves, and continue for 2km (1 mile) to the second set of such signs for a left-hand turn; Château La Rame is 1.5km (1 mile) up the hill at la Rame. Yves Armand's old house covers a very modern winery, a source of fine Ste-Croix-du-Mont sweet whites, Bordeaux Blanc Sec, Bordeaux Rosé, and Premières Côtes Rouge. From Ste-Croix-du-Mont take the D10 to St-Maixant where you turn left for Verdelais. Go through the town with the basilica on the right, and the cellars of Domaines Tich et Grava are on the left, with a red gate. Jean Fonteyreaud's two vineyards lie in Ste-Croix-du-Mont and Verdelais. His dry Rosé du Cabernet offers a more aromatic, refreshing, and ageable alternative to the more commonly found Merlot-dominated pink Bordeaux.

Also worth a visit

Other estates worth visiting for their impressive château buildings include the nineteenth-century Château du Grand Mouëys (tel: 05 57 97 04 40) in Capian; Château Lamothe de Haux (tel: 05 57 34 53 00, www.château-lamothe.com) in Haux with its large underground barrel cellars; the palatial eighteenth-century Château de Plassan (tel: 05 56 67 53 16, www.chateauplassan.fr) in Tabanac, whose château and grounds have been beautifully restored over the last twenty years; and the seventeenth-century Château de Ricaud (tel: 05 56 62 66 16) in Loupiac.

Feeling festive?

The locals round here are keen on festivals. You can ask at the local tourist offices (*see* p.125) for details on local festivals, both general town ones and wine-specific ones. World-weary

ABOVE An impressively thick vine trunk, over sixty years old.

wine tourists might find the town festivals cheaper, and less contrived. Town festivals include: Baurech, July 13; Bouliac, first weekend in June; Medieval weekend in Bouliac, first weekend in September; Cadillac, May 1 and last weekend in August; Cambes, July 14; Carignan de Bordeaux, third weekend in May; giant omelette-making, Easter Monday in Haux; Le Tourne, on July 14; Paillet, second week in June; fire-stations' balls in Quinsac, July 13 to commemorate the eve of the 1789 Revolution; Rions street festival, beginning of July; Rions firework display, July 13; St-Caprais-de-Bordeaux firework display, July 14; St-Germain-de-Grave, last Sunday in July; lamb festival in St-Germain-de-Grave, Ascension Day (May/June, depending on the date of Easter); Ste-Croix-du-Mont, third weekend in June.

Wine-specific festivals include: Latresne, end September; St-Caprais-de-Bordeaux, October; Ste-Croix-du-Mont, fourth weekend in May. There is a Saturday morning market in Cadillac.

P. Côtes, Cadillac, Loupiac, and Ste-C. wine facts

The Premières Côtes cover just over 4,000ha of mainly red wine vines in thirty-seven villages. Four main wine styles are produced: reds labelled as Premières Côtes de Bordeaux Rouge; dry whites labelled Bordeaux Blanc Sec; sweetish whites labelled Premières Côtes de Bordeaux Blanc; and very sweet whites labelled Cadillac, Loupiac or Ste-Croix-du-Mont. The deep pink wines called *clairet*, are said to have been invented in the Premières Côtes, and can be quite substantial.

WHERE TO STAY

St James
3 place Camille Hostein
33270 Bouliac
Tel: 05 57 97 06 00
reception@saint-james-bouliac.com
Modern, elegant hotel, popular with celebrities, with views across the Garonne. Try the *"retour du marché"* menu for value. The gastronomic menu is for serious foodies.

Château de La Tour
33410 Cadillac sur Garonne
Tel: 05 56 76 92 00
hotel@chathotel-delatour.com
Hotel rooms open onto a wooded park. There's a sauna and jacuzzi. The inconsistent restaurant is closed Friday evenings and weekends.

Entre-Deux-Mers

E ntre-Deux-Mers is the vast sweep of land "between the two seas", or waters, of the Dordogne and Garonne. At 80km (50 miles) in length and up to 30km (20 miles) wide, this is Bordeaux's biggest wine region and the one where wine tourists have the most chance of haggling successfully for a bargain, especially if they have an empty car boot to fill.

Bulk bargains

Bargain hunters could do worse than to show up at the cooperatives that still dominate the region. The Union de Producteurs at Rauzan (tel: 05 57 84 13 22) is Bordeaux's largest co-op, and is open Monday to Saturday; Sunday in July and August. You can purchase cubitaners (a square plastic container with a tap), or take your own. The co-op's own labels are Château du Charron and the better Le Prestige des Vignerons.

Other cooperatives in Entre Deux Mers who are happy to receive visitors and sell wines direct include the Cave Cooperative de Vinification de Quinsac (89 Pranzac, 33360

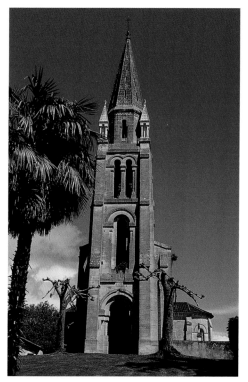

Quinsac, tel: 05 56 20 86 09, cave.de.quinsac@wanadoo.fr) which specilialises in the deep pink *clairet* style; the ugly looking but underrated Cave Cooperative de Ruch (chais de Vaure, 33350 Ruch, tel: 05 57 40 54 09, chais-de-vaure@wanadoo.fr); and the immense SCV Cellier de la Bastide at Sauveterre de Guyenne (33540 Sauveterre de Guyenne, tel: 05 56 61 55 20, administratif @cellierdelabastide. com). Or, you could contact the Fédération des Coopératives Vinicoles d'Aquitaine (6 Parvis des Chartrons, Cité Mondiale, 33075 Bordeaux Cédex, tel: 05 56 00 81 00, www.fcva.com) which has details of all Bordeaux's fifty-two cooperatives.

Architectural pleasures

Local wine co-ops tend to be anything but architectural masterpieces, so if it's architecture that interests you, concentrate on the region's many fine châteaux, such as the immense one at Vayres, and on its manor houses, its Romanesque churches and its other religious buildings, such as the monastery at Blasimon and the ruined Benedictine abbey at La Sauve-Majeure.

The terraces and gardens of the Château de Vayres run down to the Dordogne river (tel: 05 56 84 96 59; open all year round; visits by appointment with fee payable). The ruined Romanesque abbey at St-Ferme; the Romanesque church at Targon in Bordeaux-Haut-Benauge and that at Loupiac, classified a historic monument, are among the region's finest examples. The fortress at Langoiran overlooking the Gironde dates from 1250 and has been renovated (tel: 05 56 67 12 00).

ABOVE *The former railway station at Espiet, now a restaurant.*

LEFT *The rich farmland behind Civrac-sur-Dordogne's church is used by nurserymen to propagate young vines.*

Entre-Deux-Mers may be a vast region, but it contains France's smallest village in Castelmoron-d'Albret, which is about the same size as three soccer pitches. Its pretty houses lie on a limestone ridge with great views between Sauveterre-de-Guyenne and Monségur.

Getting there

By car, entering the Entre-Deux-Mers region means crossing either the Dordogne or Garonne rivers. For crossing points over the Garonne *see* the Premières Côtes chapter (p.125), or if you are arriving from the Dordogne department via Marmande you can enter Entre-Deux-Mers by the bridge at La Réole.

If you are coming from the north and thus across the Dordogne, there are bridges at Libourne (into the Graves de Vayres sub-region), at Branne if you are coming from St-Emilion, at Castillon-la-Bataille if you are coming from the Côtes de Castillon and Côtes de Francs, or at Ste-Foy-la-Grande if coming from the Dordogne department town of Port-Ste-Foy (*see* p.127). Bus services from Bordeaux on CITRAM Aquitaine to Entre-Deux-Mers are sporadic, with no services at all to Ste-Foy-la-Grande and La Réole, and only one per day to Pellegrue and Sauveterre-la-Guyenne. However, there are seven per day to Branne (Ligne 402) and thirteen per day to Cadillac (Ligne 501).

Rail services from Bordeaux St-Jean to Entre-Deux-Mers on the SNCF are also limited. Only the towns of Ste-Foy-la-Grande (six trains per day, taking between one hour and two hours thirty minutes depending on connections) and Le Réole (one per hour, taking thirty to sixty minutes) are served. You can stop at St-Emilion and Castillon-la-Bataille on the service to Ste-Foy.

Your best bet for this region is car hire. Ask at local tourist offices for the best deals (*see* right).

LOCAL INFORMATION

Créon Tourist Office
7 bis rue du Docteur Fauché
33670 Créon
Tel: 05 56 23 23 00

La Réole Tourist Office
1 place de la Libération
33190 La Réole
Tel: 05 56 61 13 55

Ste-Foy-la-Grande T. Office
102 rue de la République
33220 Ste-Foy-la-Grande
Tel: 05 57 46 03 00

Monségur Tourist Office
place Darniche
33580 Monségur
Tel: 05 56 61 60 12

Travelling around

With such a vast area, we have devised two routes, one leaving from Bordeaux, the other based on the more central Branne.

Route one: approximately 80km (50 miles) in length, from Bordeaux's Pont de Pierre we go through Beychac-et-Caillau, Arveyres, Génissac, Moulon, Tizac de Curton, St-Quentin-de-Baron, Créon and La Sauve-Majeure, back to Créon, then to the hamlet of Lorient, and back to Bordeaux.

Route two: about 100km (65 miles) long, this takes us from Branne to St-Jean-de-Blaignac, Pujols, Ste-Radegon-de-Juillac, Gensac, Ste-Foy-la-Grande, Les-Lèves-et Thoumeyragues, Pellegrue, Ste-Ferme, Monségur, La Réole, Gironde-sur-Dropt, Morizes, and back to Gironde-sur-Dropt for St-Macaire, Gornac, Lugasson, and back to Branne.

Route one: depth, value, and a desirable pink

Leave Bordeaux city over the Pont de Pierre and get on the N89, direction Libourne. Go through Beychac-et-Caillau. After 25km (15 miles) you reach Arveyres where you turn right, onto the D18 to Génissac. After 5km (3 miles) as you leave Génissac for Moulon, Château Belle-Garde appears on the left (*see right*). The château's affable owner, Eric Duffau, runs a firework business

Entre-Deux-Mers: route one
Allow half a day or more, especially if you plan a museum trip

Entre-Deux Mers: route two
As above, half-a-day to a day should suffice, depending on your non-wine plans

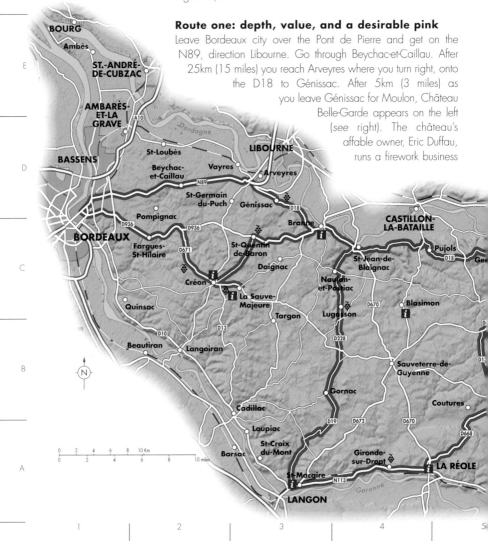

when he is not making inky reds and value-for-money dry whites based on equal proportions of Sauvignon Blanc and Sémillon.

From Belle-Garde carry on another 5km (3 miles) towards Branne, but at the T-junction with the D936, instead of turning left into Branne, turn right to Tizac de Curton and St-Quentin-de-Baron. After 6km (4 miles) Château de Sours is on the right (see right). Scot Esmé Johnstone and his wife Sara produce one of Bordeaux's most sought-after pink wines from a vineyard first planted just after the 1789 Revolution.

Around Créon

From St-Quentin-de-Baron, get on the D121 for the 8km (5-mile) drive to Créon. The road crosses the Gestas, one of the many streams draining the Entre-Deux-Mers plateau. In Créon, head east on the D671 towards La Sauve-Majeure, but after less than 1.6km (1 mile) take the right turn at the roundabout with the D13. Château Thieuley is almost immediately on the left (see "châteaux to visit"). Francis Courselle is handing over this well-run estate to his daughter Marie.

Get back on the D671 to Créon and go through Créon on the way to Bordeaux. Just over 3.5km (2 miles) after Créon, in the hamlet of Lorient, there is a stone cross on the right. At this point, on the left, is the Chemin de Farizeau, at the end of which is Château Farizeau (see right). André and Nicole Moreau like their vines to grow extra-high: more leaves mean more sugar in the grapes, and richer wines. Their varietal Cabernet Franc reds taste of homemade jam with a sprig of mint.

From Château Farizeau it is just over 24km (15 miles) back to Bordeaux. Return there by taking the D671 towards Salleboeuf and turn left at La Planteyre onto the D936 to Bordeaux.

Route two: chewy reds, winning whites, and sublime sweeties

The second route begins in Branne. Get here either from Bordeaux (see route one) or from St-Emilion. Turn right just before the Branne bridge on the D18 to St-Jean-de-Blaignac, and stay on this road via Pujols, Ste-Radegonde, Juillac, and Gensac where the Ste-Foy appellation begins. At Eynesse, you join the D130 to Ste-Foy-la-Grande (40km/25 miles) from Branne.

CHATEAUX IN ENTRE-DEUX-MERS

Château Belle-Garde
Monplaisir
33420 Génissac
Tel: 05 57 24 49 12 *(D3)*
www.duffau.eric@wanadoo.fr

Domaine de Bouillerot
33190 Gironde-sur-Dropt
Tel: 05 56 71 46 04 *(A4)*

Château Farizeau
21 Chemin de Fer
L'Orient
33670 Sadirac
Tel: 05 56 30 61 46 *(C2)*

Château le Rait
33220 Les Lèves-et-Thoumeyragues
Tel: 05 57 41 22 29 *(C6)*

Château Roquefort
33760 Lugasson
Tel: 05 56 23 97 48 *(C4)*
www.chateau-roquefort@wanadoo.fr

Château de Sours
33750 St-Quentin-de-Baron
Tel: 05 57 24 10 81 *(D3)*
www.chateaudesours.com

Château Thieuley
33670 La Sauve-Majeure
Tel: 05 56 23 00 01 *(C3)*
www.chateau.thieuley@wandoo.fr

PRICES: moderate

You can either go into Ste-Foy, and back out again, or at the Pont de la Beauze turn right onto the D672, direction Pellegrue. Just south of Les-Lèves-et-Thoumeyragues, 8km (5 miles) from Ste-Foy, and on the left, you will see Château le Rait (*see* p.133). Claude Capoul's organic vineyard can look chaotic, but the wines show a tidy mix of fruit and oak.

Back to Entre-Deux-Mers

Continue on the D672 for 11km (7 miles) to Pellegrue. Here you leave the Ste-Foy appellation and get back into Entre-Deux-Mers as you pick up the D16 for 16km (10 miles) through Ste-Ferme to Monségur. Then take the D668 to La Réole (24km/15 miles).

Follow the N113 for 5km (3 miles) to Gironde-sur-Dropt, and as you leave the town turn right on the D15 towards Morizès. After 1.5km (1 mile), past Paysan and at La Combe, turn left. Domaine de Bouillerot's cellar is 50 metres on the left (*see* right). The local red clay soil here is used to good effect both by the local brickworks, and by Thierry and Véronique Bos as the perfect foundation for red wines. Their handpicked dry and sweet whites excel.

Rambling to Branne

From Gironde-sur-Dropt drive the 12km (8 miles) to the town of St-Macaire and the heart of the Côtes de Bordeaux St-Macaire appellation. From here take the D19, direction Branne, but after 11km (7 miles) at Terrey-de-Castel turn right onto the D230 to Gornac.

In Gornac, get on the D228 to Lugasson where Château Roquefort is signposted southeast of the town (*see* p.133). This slightly rambling estate produces chewy reds from vineyards containing Gallo-Roman remains. Head back to Branne via St-Jean-de-Blaignac via Bellefond and Jugazan on the D119/D119E. There is also a windmill in Gornac which affords a good view over the local countryside.

Fortifications and museums

If you are staying in this area you should visit some fortified towns, the *bastides*. From 1152 this part of France came under English rule and later, during the Hundred Years' War, it became frontier territory.

The towns of Créon, Ste-Foy-la-Grande, Monségur, Blasimon, Sauveterre-de-Guyenne, Cadillac (*see* Premières Côtes p.124), and Pellegrue were fortified, acting as political, troop- and tax-raising centres for either the French or English kings. Contact local tourist offices if you want to explore these fortifications in detail. If museums are your thing, then don't miss the postal museum in St-Macaire (Musée postal d'Aquitaine,

15 place Mercadiou, 33490 St Macaire (tel: 05 56 63 08 81), a must for stamp enthusiasts. Fans of literature should visit the former home of writer François Mauriac (1885–1970) at Château Malagar in St-Maixant (Centre François Mauriac, Domaine de Malagar, 33490 St-Maixant, tel: 05 57 98 17 16), which is also a working winery.

In May various commemorative events are staged on the 35km (22-miles) route along the N10 between Bordeaux and Malagar (see www.route fmauriac.org for details).

Foodies should contact the museum at Domaine Belloc in Sadirac (33670 Sadirac, tel: 05 56 30 61 00, www. ohlegumesoublies.com) which organizes conferences, fairs, and tastings of "forgotten fruits and vegetables" in spring and autumn, and has a child-friendly exhibition illustrating the history of what we eat.

ABOVE *Fortifications in towns like Monségur were built by the English when they ruled this part of France, 800 years ago.*

Sadirac's pottery museum, the Maison de la Poterie in the town centre (tel: 05 56 30 60 03) contains pieces excavated from Sadirac dating from antiquity, and organizes educational mornings, the latter mainly geared towards French kids on school trips. In the third week of June thirty local potters hold an exhibition and sale (email: ceramic-agap@wanadoo.fr).

In La Réole four museums are crammed into a former tobacco-processing factory (19 avenue Gabriel Chaigne, 33190 La Réole, tel: 05 56 61 29 25), one has agricultural machinery, one has second world war tanks, uniforms and the like, one covers railway history, and one is an automobile museum.

Those interested in astronomy and astrophysics can visit the Bordeaux Observatory in Floirac, just across the Garonne from Bordeaux (2 rue de l'Observatoire, 33270 Floirac, tel: 05 57 77 61 00, www.obs.u-bordeaux1.fr), or attend a seminar.

Better by balloon

You can hire a piloted hot air balloon from Aquitaine Terroirs (84 rue Montesquieu, 33500 Libourne, tel: 05 57 74 19 10, www.aquitaineterroirs.com, lambert.voyages@ wanadoo.fr).

Tours are usually over the Libournais but if you can find somewhere to take off in Entre-Deux-Mers, Aquitaine Terroirs will be happy to oblige. Allow up to four hours per trip, including one hour to blow up and deflate, and one to two hours flying time. Most flights take place in early morning or evenings.

RIGHT *Some châteaux become too expensive to maintain, especially when any spare cash is being invested in the vines.*

Wine fairs

At the tourist offices you can ask about local wine fairs (foires aux vins) in La Reole (early June), Sauveterre-de-Guyenne (end of July) and Créon (early November).

During the last weekend in March every other year the Ste-Croix-du-Mont wineries hold an open day. Contact the local winegrower's union for details. Ste-Foy-la-Grande holds a fair on March 20 and November 20, focused on local wines and foods. The Saturday market here is one of France's most beautiful. St-Pierre d'Aurillac hosts a shad (a herring-like fish) festival during the last weekend in June, with traditional shad-based meals and a ball on the Saturday, plus a free music festival on Sunday. Sauveterre-de-Guyenne has a food and wine fair during the second-last weekend of July, and a medieval day on the second last Saturday in August.

In the third weekend in July, Créon hosts a Night of Art and the Bicycle in which artists and craftsmen exhibit along a designated cycle route (email the Créon tourist office on www.otcreon@wanadoo.fr for details).

In September, La Réole hosts a harvest festival with tastings of grape juice and young wines, plus locally grown and barbecued sweet chestnuts.

Not worried about your waistline? Check out the "Foire au Gras" or "Fat Festival" in Monségur in December and February.

Entre-Deux-Mers wine facts

The Entre-Deux-Mers region as a whole produces over 400 million bottles of wine each year, most of it red. Entre-Deux-Mers produces reds under the basic Bordeaux and Bordeaux-Supérieur appellations, the latter being "superior" only because it contains a mite more alcohol. Dry whites, much improved in recent years, are labelled Bordeaux Blanc Sec or Entre-Deux-Mers. A small sub-region called Haut-Benauge, at the geographic heart of Entre-Deux-Mers centres around nine towns of which Targon is the largest. Haut-Benauge is said to produce this region's finest dry whites, because of the presence of fossilized oyster shells in the soils. These shells are supposed to give the white wines extra elegance, aroma, and flavour. Dry whites are bottled (rather cumbersomely) as Entre-Deux-Mers-Bordeaux-Haut-Benauge Blanc Sec, with medium-dry styles labelled Bordeaux-Haut-Benauge Blanc Moelleux.

The other sub-regions here include the insignificant Graves de Vayres (one million bottles) which faces Libourne across the Dordogne, from the communes of Vayres and Arveyres, the latter on the main N89 Libourne-Bordeaux road; Ste-Foy-Bordeaux (three million bottles) covers a score of villages around Ste-Foy-la-Grande in eastern Entre-Deux-Mers, an area with several good organic growers (ask Claude Capoul of Château le Rait for organic contacts, see p.133). Ste-Foy is bordered to the east by the Dordogne department, with the rich cuisine of the Périgord such as pate, foie gras, and truffles; and Côtes-de-Bordeaux-St-Macaire (400,000 bottles), known historically for sweetish whites.

The St-Macaire region will forever be associated with the post-impressionist painter Henri de Toulouse-Lautrec (1864–1901), who died at Château Malromé (see right) and is buried in the cemetery at Verdelais. This town was an old pilgrim destination, and above the high altar of the church's basilica is a supposedly miracle-working fourteenth-century wooden cross.

INDEX